DATE DUE

JAN 04 2010			

Demco, Inc. 38-293

24/7

How Cell Phones and the Internet Change the Way We Live, Work, and Play

24/7

How Cell Phones and the Internet Change the Way We Live, Work, and Play

Jarice Hanson

PRAEGER

Westport, Connecticut
London

Library of Congress Cataloging-in-Publication Data

Hanson, Jarice.
24/7 : how cell phones and the Internet change the way we live, work, and play / Jarice
Hanson.
    p. cm.
    Includes bibliographical references and index.
    ISBN–13: 978–0–275–99333–7 (alk. paper)
    1. Cellular telephones–Social aspects.   2. Internet–Social aspects.   3. Interpersonal
communication–Technological innovations–Social aspects.   4. Social
interaction–Technological innovations.   5. Social change. I. Title. II. Title: Cell
phones and the Internet change the way we live, work, and play.   III. Title: Twenty-four
seven.
  HE9713.H365   2007
  303.48'33–dc22   2007018524

British Library Cataloguing in Publication Data is available.

Library of Congress Catalog Card Number: 2007018524
ISBN-13: 0–978–0–275–99333–7
ISBN-10: 0–275–99333–7

First published in 2007

Praeger Publishers, 88 Post Road West, Westport, CT 06881
An imprint of Greenwood Publishing Group, Inc.
www.praeger.com

Printed in the United States of America

The paper used in this book complies with the
Permanent Paper Standard issued by the National
Information Standards Organization (Z39.48–1984).

10 9 8 7 6 5 4 3 2 1

To some of the people who have enriched my life in ways
I never thought possible: Bernard J. Brommel, mentor and friend;
Adele Oppenheim, explorer and guide; Frank S. Aronson, who makes
me laugh and maintains my link to the digital world;
and to my students, who continually challenge me to explore and
explain why things are the way they are.

Contents

We're all so busy—busy—busy! Who among us hasn't tried to make a New Year's Eve resolution to make more time for themselves? We live in a time in which so many technologies offer us new levels of control over our lives—from comfortable cars designed to accommodate our changing lifestyles to personal computers and cell phones, we now have more mobility and more choices in how and when we communicate with others than any time in history. It would seem logical that we could use these technologies to make our lives easier, so why do we continue to feel so much stress?

From the ability to work from home by using the Internet to keeping track of the kids by cell phone, the lives of Americans have embraced a range of technologies that have changed the way we communicate, how we communicate, and what we communicate. From one perspective, cell phones and the Internet still merely offer us a greater number of alternatives for how we do things that other technologies had already allowed us to do; wired phones, mail through the post office, libraries, radio, television, and film all allowed us access to other people, to information, and to entertainment. Now, however, we can do everything we used to do faster, either through cell phones or the Internet, or a combination of both.

The theme of this cultural history has to do with how these technologies have created an environment in which expectations of instant communication, information, and entertainment are fully accessible twenty-four hours a day, seven days a week. While apparently promising us greater control over our time and the ability to engage in a more mobile, individually centered society, the inherent characteristics of the technology and the way people choose to use them results in what I call an *illusion* of control that conditions us to have expectations that are often unmet. Indeed, the history of communication and information technologies shows that technologies promise much, but have many unintended consequences, and the relationship between technological innovation and social use results in new behaviors, attitudes, and values.

Often, as I was working on this manuscript, I would have conversations with people who asked what the book was about. When I told them the title, I would inevitably get the following response: eyes would roll, heads would nod, and everyone wanted to tell me a story of how either cell phones or the Internet, or both, had made their lives more complicated and added more stress and more work, or how something critical to them had inevitably gone wrong because they relied on one or both of the technologies. But when pressed, only one person out of more than a dozen actually made the decision to throw away his cell phone, and only two had canceled home Internet service. Two of the three individuals were over the age of fifty. When I posed the question to my college-age students about whether they could choose not to use their cell phones or the Internet, they looked at me as though I had suggested they give up breathing. In researching the material for this book and consulting individuals of all ages, it quickly became apparent to me that there were multiple realities at work about the role cell phones and the Internet played in Americans' lives, but that everyone understood that these technologies were the crucial tools to understanding how our culture is changing, and for whom.

My goal is to make us think about activities in which we engage daily, but seldom really consider, so that we can assess the impact of cell phones and the Internet on the values that make us uniquely "American." Many of my sources come from both scholarly and popular research on the impact of technologies and social change, and how these technologies and services continue to influence the way we organize our lives and think about our status in the world. Popular books and magazines often address those elements of social change that demonstrate either surface-level changes, or attempt to explain *how* technology is fostering specific changes in traditional ways of doing things, while more scholarly approaches ground us in more complex, theoretical and methodological approaches to the broader impact of social and cultural change. If there is one uniting theme in most popular and academic literature, it is that *if* we can understand the potential of technology to change the way we work, live, or play, we can control the impact of these technologies in our lives. The position outlined in this book is that though we may think cell phones and the Internet give us greater control over our lives, they really give us an *illusion* of control that provides an even more complex set of social changes that deeply affect our beliefs, attitudes, and values. In turn, we bring a set of expectations to the experience of using these technologies, but those expectations are often unmet, and other experiences substitute for what we had hoped to have gained.

As we examine the technologies and their ability to influence how, why, and when we communicate, we can see how they influence our senses of time and space by influencing our attitudes of appropriate public and private behaviors. At the same time, the portability and availability of communication through cell phones and the Internet have blurred traditional concepts of public and private activities.

What is particularly important about cell phones and the Internet is that both are responsible for changing long-held beliefs in American culture about what binds us together in a common culture. "Mass society," "mass media," and "mass culture" are the primary victims of these two technologies and of the way they have influenced the direction of American life and culture. The role of the individual and the growing fragmentation of channels of information that once bound us together in a society that fostered a common set of socially constructed beliefs, attitudes, values, and the expectations that we commonly held, have changed because our communication technologies today have accelerated the pace of social change. Long-held values of appropriate behaviors in private and public places have come under attack. Issues of time and space have changed the way we think of ourselves as individuals, and as members of society. Both cell phones and the Internet can be wonderful technologies for speed, efficiency, and access to things we want or need, but at the same time they can also be the cause of stress, anxiety, and unhappiness, and ultimately, they can change the way we think about privacy, social relations, and democratic practices.

The ultimate result of having technologies that both allow us, and sometimes require us to communicate twenty-four hours a day, seven days a week, is that our traditional ways of thinking about how we live, work, and play are changing. By understanding the nature of these changes we can make better decisions about how we, as individuals and in a collective society, carve a future for our children and ourselves.

Every chapter in this book deals with the nature of how American culture is changing in response to the way cell phones and the Internet have become critical technologies in contemporary life. Moving from the broader questions of who might be most affected by use of these new technologies to how cell phones and the Internet extend traditional media forms to new audiences and activities, the chapters develop themes that show how American culture is absorbing the shock waves of using cell phones and the Internet for an increasing number of uses. Questions of the time and space-altering issues, and the blurring of public and private activities, form the themes that demonstrate how these two technologies are leading Americans to expect more immediate responses to their needs, a belief that they have greater control over their lives, and how substitutions of mediated reality have influenced the quality of personal interactions.

The first three chapters of the book outline shifts in American culture from ideas of mass society to the importance of niche audiences, how traditional technologies led consumers to have expectations of how to use cell phone and Internet, and how the relationship of innovation, social use, and time in history forms the basis of a shared cultural history. Chapters 4 through 8 emphasize different aspects of how the time and space characteristics of the technology, the blurring of public and private uses, and the integration of social uses of these technologies have provided opportunities to see how American attitudes and behaviors are changing, leading us toward a new set of values. The concluding chapter examines how some specific uses of cell phones and the Internet have already given rise to new attitudes, behaviors, and values, and outlines the direction of cultural change we may well want to consider as we continue to use these technologies for greater use of communication and information.

CHAPTER OUTLINES

Chapter 1 introduces the idea of communication and information access twenty-four hours a day, seven days a week, and looks at how technologies have characteristics that specifically influence the nature of time and space, and public and private issues. The nature of understanding communication "revolutions" makes the case that it is hard to predict how technologies will be used, and by whom—but we can look to that history to see how institutions and social practices have evolved as the result of technological change, specifically within the United States. The breakdown of the traditional "mass" media and "mass society" show how these technologies have emphasized notions of niche audiences and how the individualization of choices of content and choices of technologies has set the backdrop for entrepreneurial activity in information delivery via cell phones and the Internet.

Chapter 2 addresses the direct precursors to cell phones and the Internet and examines how traditional telephony provided a model used for both business and social communication. It examines the intentional and unintentional effects of creating a wired system of voiced communication in the United States and provides a foundation for what cultural history offers us as a means of understanding social change.

Chapter 3 looks at who uses cell phones and the Internet in the United States and what divisions exist in our society in terms of knowledge, expertise, and experimentation with new uses of cell phones and the Internet. Questions of access to the technologies further underscore the premise that both cell phones and the Internet are influenced by perceived need by different age groups, as well as persons of differential income. With a sociological grounding, the concepts of the digital divide and social background are examined to consider who can use these technologies, and for what purposes. Using traditional popular terms, this chapter looks at the "haves" and "have nots," but also raises the issue that some people actively choose not to use them and might be considered "don't wants."

Chapter 4 specifically focuses on the issue of control—how some individuals lose personal control over their use of the Internet and cell phones. These dysfunctional applications outline how issues of time and control can result in addictive behaviors and how certain uses of these technologies in private places can lead some people to behaviors that might not otherwise be possible. Video gaming provides a study of how some individuals lose themselves in cyberspace and how issues of anonymity and identity formation can take place in this special, nonphysical world.

Chapter 5 specifically focuses on the how cell phones and the Internet can be used to create opportunities for a greater exchange of viewpoints. Engagement in digital democracy is one of the great promises of interactive electronic technology, and this chapter addresses the current use of some applications of public information exchange, such as blogging and podcasting and questions what happens when we rely on technology as a component for enhancing political participation.

Chapter 6 focuses on social networking and the way individuals regard cell phones and the Internet as secure, personal technologies. When people believe that they use these forms for secure, intimate exchange of information, they often find that their privacy can be invaded by a number of agents monitoring personal information. By focusing on the issues of loss of privacy as we use these technologies for more personal purposes, and the problems of identity theft, through cookies, adware, spyware, viruses, and other by-products of online communication, and the social control exercised by cell phones, we examine the idea of "placelessness" in a more technologically conceived "community."

Chapter 7 asks important questions about copyright and intellectual property, our knowledge of the validity of information, and the accuracy of the information we access—and whether we are up to the challenge of determining fact from fiction or opinion. New collections of information, like Wikipedia, raise problems for the fragmentary nature of information and validity. Questions of anonymity in using cell phones and the Internet are measured against traditional policies and laws.

Chapter 8 looks at some of the artifacts of an earlier time, such as public telephone booths, and traditional media industries to see how our environment and our media landscapes are in transition. In particular, it focuses on what happened to legacy media industries as distribution forms migrate to the Internet and to cell phones and how new business models reflect a range of different perspectives that lend credence to younger individuals' skills.

Chapter 9 focuses on the future and how cell phones and Internet services are likely to continue to shape social practices in different environments in America and abroad. It questions whether greater access to technology will call for a new concept of the global village.

Acknowledgments

I am indebted to several people who have not only contributed to the ideas that shaped this book, but also to the Verizon Corporation of Pennsylvania. Their generous endowment of the Verizon Chair in Telecommunications at the School of Communications and Theater at Temple University in Philadelphia made it possible for me to spend the time to think and write. Throughout my tenure as the Verizon Chair, I have been given the ultimate flexibility and total freedom to choose my projects. I have received unwavering support, and my decisions on how to spend my time have never been questioned. That type of luxury is rare, especially in the world of academe, and I thank Jim Reed, director of public affairs, for his constant good humor and support. Both James V. O'Rourke, president of Verizon Pennsylvania during my first two years as Verizon Chair, and William B. Petersen, current president, respected my choice of projects and demonstrated gracious attention.

I'm equally indebted to Concetta Stewart, dean of the School of Communications and Theater at Temple, a dynamic administrator who gives enormous freedom to her faculty and demonstrates that generosity and trust are the best qualities to have in a leader. Tom Jacobson, senior associate dean for academic affairs, has been a trusted friend and colleague as well as providing an important link from past to present. To my graduate research assistants who put up with cryptic directions, strange schedules, and half-baked ideas, I thank you and hope that you've learned something in the process of multitasking and the power of fragmented thinking; Dandan Liu, Ph.D., Margaret Griffith, and Leanne Chang each contributed enormously to this project as well as many others.

Hilary Claggett saw the raw ideas behind this book and gave helpful comments and criticism. She believed in this project before I did. If there is such a thing as making a friend by e-mail, she's the real deal. Holly Givens, true friend, read and reread this manuscript, giving many hours to thoughtfully questioning the content, pointing out non sequitors and errant commas. For a stand-up comic, she knows her punctuation.

Most of all, thanks to Frank S. Aronson, who put up with hours of my complaints, my nervous energy, and my computer frustration. A true partner in every sense of the word, he always seemed to know when I needed a laugh, a hug, or to be left alone. His patience, good humor, and support were and are invaluable.

One

24/7: Anytime, Anywhere

Many people are feeling a strange vibration in the air these days. This constant invisible hum has to do with those who rush past others, avoiding eye contact and babbling to themselves. Some of these folks have large growths protruding from one of their ears and something resembling a short straw bifurcating their cheeks and inching toward their mouths, like an alien tentacle reaching to suck the life force from them. Then there are those who sit on public benches, buses, or subway cars, tapping their thumbs on miniscule keyboards and protected by an invisible bubble from any human contact. All of these people seem oblivious to the world around them.

Not many years ago, people in public who appeared to be talking to themselves or to be fixated on small devices might have been thought to be psychotic. In a way, these people are experiencing a *technological psychosis*, in that the technology intrudes on the reality of the world around them. Of course, the two technologies most associated with these behaviors are the cell phone and the laptop computer, the latter of which probably uses a wireless connection to the Internet. Or, a person might be using a personal digital assistant (PDA) such as a BlackBerry or Treo, or a multifunction smart phone that combines the features of both a cell phone and a minicomputer. As we move increasingly toward a world of wireless phone transmissions and wireless Internet access, this combination of forces is changing the way we do things and changing the industries that just a few years ago specialized in entertainment and communication services. When you shop for a new cell phone today, you have to consider not just a variety of devices that make phone calls, but also whether you want a camera and what type of picture resolution you'd prefer, what text-messaging capabilities you want, the number of audio and video features, how many gaming possibilities you'd like, and what other digital functions you could use.

Increasingly, cell phone calls and computer communications, whether over personal computer, laptop, or handheld device with multiple functionality, are being transmitted over the Internet in a wireless form, giving users greater mobility and allowing them to work, socialize, and interact with others anyplace where there is wireless service available. Work is no longer confined to the office, playing games can take place alone or with anonymous participants in cyberspace, and daily life can incorporate multiple functions from different locations. For many, the typical nine-to-five workday is becoming a distant memory, and the types of activities formerly associated with "home," "work," and "leisure" are no longer clearly separated. There is some irony in thinking that using cell phones and the Internet gives us more flexibility about where we go and how we control our time, but at the same time, many people report that they feel more stress in their lives, rather than less. Could these two technologies be contributing to more stress, rather than simplifying or facilitating our lives?

Everyone has a strong opinion about cell phones. Many people complain that the cell phone is an annoyance, but then claim they couldn't live without one. The cell phone is not just a more portable version of our traditional wired telephone. It is a small, portable technology that allows us to make phone calls and participate in a wide range of media interactions anywhere, anytime (as long as we're in range of a cell tower). It is actually remarkable that in a period of about ten years, cell phones have become a "must-have" technology for many, despite the often-poor reception quality or unreliability of cell phones, the need to remember to charge them, and their extra cost. In the United States, where 92.9 percent of the population already has access to a telephone,[1] the growth of the less reliable and more expensive cell phone is nothing short of a phenomenon.

Although efforts to develop radio made it possible to transmit wireless telephone messages as early as 1909,[2] there was no profitable market for wireless telephony in those days. The first commercial cell phones weren't introduced until 1985, but they didn't become really popular until 1995. By 2005, the number of new cell phones surpassed the number of land lines in the United States,[3] and two-thirds of American adults now own cell phones.[4] Despite their presence, their users are often ridiculed because of the way they use cell phones, particularly in public places. Social etiquette and new rules for how and where it might be appropriate to use cell phones are still controversial and are being socially negotiated.

Why people use cell phones and the Internet often reflects a belief that these technologies will give users greater control over their lives. What people rarely recognize is how their personal style of communication changes, and how communication habits become part of a daily routine. Callers often make calls when it is convenient for them, without giving a thought to where the person they're calling might be at that time, feeling that just leaving a message is as good as talking with someone. Some people work with others online and may even feel that they know the person with whom they communicate, even though they've never had a conversation or have a sense of what the person looks like. Even shopping or playing games can be enjoyable experiences on the Internet—but none of these activities bring someone into direct face-to-face interaction with others, raising the question of what type of communication or interaction takes place when there's no sense of a person's *body*.

Personal habits also condition people to use communication technologies in particular ways. Checking cell phone messages or answering e-mail first thing in the morning is now as much of a routine for many as having a cup of coffee or brushing your teeth. Getting news or music over the Internet is convenient and can be done while sending e-mail, reading the latest celebrity gossip, or working from home, all over the Internet. Who your "friends" are can be listed in an available directory on a cell phone or on any number of personal social networking sites on the Internet. When a cell phone is programmed to block calls from anyone who hasn't been entered into an "approved" call list, or someone removes your name from their roster of "friends," the number of interactions on either technology are limited. There is no surprise that many people claim that the more we have access to communication technologies, the less we really communicate.

The Internet became a viable form of communication as early as the 1960s, but the commercial explosion of home-based Internet use started in the early 1990s. Like many technologies that seem to become second nature to a segment of the population, the Internet has developed to provide a host of services that may have been already available to people in other ways before they found their way to the online world. Many people, particularly the younger members of our society, spend hours each day negotiating the world of the Internet—time they are not spending with other forms of media or with other people. Google's acquisition of the popular Internet site YouTube, on which anyone can post video clips, made headlines in October 2006 because of the $1.65 billion (in stock) purchase price. Within two months, Verizon, Fox, CBS, and NBC announced that they, too, were collaborating on offering an Internet alternative to YouTube.[5] The television and film industries know that they've got to court the Internet crowd or lose valuable viewers of traditional media content.

At least 76 percent of American adults now use computers either at home or at work,[6] and 66 percent access the Internet from their homes.[7] More people are paying for high-speed broadband or digital subscriber line (DSL) delivery options that allow them to use a wider range of services in the home, even though these services come at a higher cost than dial-up service, wired phones, or television cable subscriptions. The ubiquity of the Internet at home as well as at the office has become more influential in changing how people access and exchange information than the wired telephone was in the twentieth century.

Sometimes cell phones and the Internet are the catalysts for social change, and sometimes they reflect social change: either way, these technologies are contributing to subtle changes in American values and to how different groups (based on age, gender, class, and race) use those changes to define individual and group identities. This book is about the changes that cell phones and the Internet—the dynamic duo—are bringing to American life, where the technologies always seem to be "on." As a cultural history, this book examines how these two technologies—separately and together—are contributing to a change in American attitudes, behaviors, and cultural values.

It is probably human nature to want to believe that all technologies make our lives easier, better, or more efficient. After all, commercials for these products and services promise us better control over the chaos of our lives. When we first start using a new technology, we experience a learning curve. For those who learn quickly, expectations for what the technology can do for us can be wonderful. Those who struggle to learn how to use the technology may experience greater stress or anxiety. Some people try something, only to realize that they don't really like or need it. But those who do master the technology tend not to notice how they begin to rely on it. The instantaneous nature of communicating with cell phones and the Internet leads us to transmit and receive information faster and with less consideration for how it might affect our lives. Our ability to connect immediately, anywhere, anytime, to someone conditions us to think of all activities in full operation twenty-four hours a day, seven days a week. That hum we feel in the air may be constant, invisible potential for immediacy—or it may well be anxiety, particularly for those who allow these technologies to infiltrate so many aspects of daily life. Or, it may accompany the unspoken reality that our daily activities, both private and public, are changing our culture in ways that we don't yet truly understand, and for that reason, we feel uncomfortable.

Is there a relationship between the growing use of cell phones and the Internet and the pressures we feel in our lives to do more, to spend more time online, and to consider using even more technology? Part of our anxiety may be caused by the instability we feel while we negotiate the new social rules, norms, and uses of technology and as we figure out how to match our expectations with what is really possible, and yet, there seems to be no turning back to a simpler time. The continuous dance between technological innovation and social use of cell phones and the Internet has influenced the way we communicate with other people and how we feel about that interaction. This leads to the logical question, If these technologies are problematic, why do so many people use them? One answer is that we can't see the immediate effects of any technological innovation for a while, but eventually we do gain perspective on the changes that have affected us. The communication scholar Marshall McLuhan once warned that all technology is invented before we have a reason to use it,[8] meaning that once we have the technology, we find ways to integrate it into our lives.

Earlier technologies give us a clue to understanding social change. The telegraph and telephone changed American culture; they united east and west coasts with a distribution form that delivered communication and messages to people and changed the way they lived, worked, and played. The wired model of communication became the backbone for telephony and the Internet, and even though we increasingly use these technologies in wireless form, the institutions, practices, and social attitudes about communication remain rooted in the structures that introduced wired communications to American culture in the late nineteenth century and all of the twentieth.

THE CHALLENGE OF ALWAYS BEING "ON"

At first it may sound like a stretch to claim that technology has the potential to shape the way we think about other things in life. After all, many of us have been led to believe that technology has no real power in itself and that it's how people use technology that matters. Neil Postman wrote a book titled *Technopoly: The Surrender of Culture to Technology*,[9] in which he explains how using technology leads us to think of everything in technological terms. According to Postman, human beings have a need to fit the pieces of their lives into something that gives the impression of coherence, and the technologies themselves structure our interests. That's why we often seek technological solutions to technological questions and why we often reach for more technology to solve the problems caused by present technologies. We may not be consciously aware of the many ways in which technology structures our thoughts, but at the unconscious level, the same characteristics that are inherent in the technology begin to creep into our daily practices. This affects both our behavior and attitudes, but also our assumptions and expectations. Throughout the twentieth century, American society embraced the belief that technology equaled progress and that if we could get technology into the hands of more people, we could all participate in the great American Dream of consuming products and enjoying better, more comfortable lives.

Now we're waking up from that dream. There are more technologies available to a wider range of people these days, and they've become easier to use, but the quality of life issues are still a problem. Many people are finding that although the Internet works wonders for communicating with others by controlling workflow or facilitating a job, there **never seems** to be enough hours in the day to get things done. Cell phones are useful tools to let someone know you're running late for a meeting, but they often are used to cover poor planning or inconsiderate actions. These wonderful inventions have done so much to liberate us from traditional ways of working or communicating with friends or family, but we often are unaware of the "speed-up" in our lives. We tend to be working more, playing less, and finding that by being always connected by phone or computer to responsibilities and obligations, our stress levels increase, rather than decrease. The technologies make it easer to react in moments, but at the same time, we can speed through tasks and ignore thinking about their consequences or their quality. It's hard to relax when the constant barrage of messages demands our attention. Like Pavlov's dog, we become conditioned to respond immediately to electronic messages. Our nerves and senses become keenly attuned, we viscerally need to respond, and we therefore contribute to the constant hum of information and message flow and exchange. People who jump to grab their cell phones when one rings in a public place, even if it isn't their own phone, know about this type of conditioning. Most people answer e-mail sequentially, and if they think they'll go back to a previous message, the message is easily forgotten. These people understand the way the technology is controlling them, too—especially when someone screams, "Didn't you get my e-mail?"

Cell phones, like many technologies we use in public, also confer a level of status for their users. The executive who uses a BlackBerry to answer e-mail during a business meeting, the person in the grocery store wearing a prominently displayed wireless earpiece while shopping, and the college student who balks at paying fifty dollars for a textbook but thinks nothing of spending two hundred dollars for the latest cell phone often justify their purchase of the technology by publicly displaying it and wordlessly boasting about their importance and technological sophistication.

On the surface, changes to the Internet may seem less obvious, but in reality they are even more profound. The ubiquity of accessing the Internet through a host of technologies and the growing functionality of cell phones to access the Internet is throwing the traditional media companies into a tizzy to find suitable content for delivery to the small video screen. Advertisers are fearful that they may lose their traditional revenue streams if they continue to promote products the old fashioned way. Subscription services that don't include ads or content that had been designed to catch someone's attention change the way people may be motivated to think about a purchase of a product. The biggest change, though, is how pop-up ads, animation, and design factors punctuate content on the computer screen, competing for attention and immediate action from the consumer, all of which can be seen more legibly on a large computer screen, but which suffers when reduced to a two-inch cell phone screen.

Whether people use cell phones and the Internet at work, in public, or for personal reasons also contributes to how "connected" they feel to other people and to their daily obligations. The portable features of cell phones and the ease of accessing the Internet in public places or over the cell phone influences peoples' attitudes and behaviors about where they can go and still remain productive. When people can be contacted wherever they are, the distinctions between personal time and obligations to work, family, or friends can seem endless. We might feel that we have greater control over our time, but the urge to be constantly in touch with others can be so stressful that consciously or unconsciously, we begin to think in Luddite terms.[10] After all, people might find it more comfortable to work from home and more convenient to buy things over the Internet, and it may be more reassuring to know that we can reach a loved one at any time of day or night, but at the same time we become primed for responding to the cell phone's ring or the computer's audio cue that something just arrived, and we may feel that whatever the message, it needs immediate attention.

Many people justify the use of these technologies by claiming that the conveniences outweigh the annoyance of listening to someone else's phone ring, or overhearing a private conversation in a public place, or feeling oppressed by e-mails that need answering. Using cell phones and the Internet in different places creates competition for attention and focus. The portability and small size of a cell phone allows people to shift attention to the technology rather than paying attention in some environments that are structured to allow a person to focus on an activity. Evidence shows that when we use a cell phone in a car, our attention is not necessarily on our driving, and accidents can occur. Personal conversations are often interrupted while someone answers a cell phone call, to the annoyance of the other person in the conversation, who feels less important in the personal interaction. Technologically savvy teens are adept at text messaging, game playing, and downloading free content, but they often do this while in class or some other inappropriate place, much to the consternation of their teachers. The intersection of the positive and negative aspects of technology results in a change in values— how we think about what we do, and how we reach a feeling of satisfaction or contentment with our present lives, or not.

TECHNOLOGICAL REVOLUTIONS AND SOCIAL CHANGE

Would we use cell phones and the Internet so readily if they didn't fit a contemporary lifestyle that attempts to pack more organizational productivity into every day? Do cell phones and the Internet really contribute to a feeling that we can control more aspects of our social environments? Few would disagree that the pace of American life has accelerated throughout the twentieth century, but how convincing is the argument that technology has contributed to this feeling of faster-paced lifestyles? It would be difficult to mount an argument that the faster pace of life is the result of cell phones and the Internet, but these technologies are undoubtedly components of the type of social change that Americans have experienced in recent years, particularly as instant communication has become more of a factor in social life. The rise of the wired communication system in the late 1800s (the long revolution) and the mobility afforded by cell phones and the Internet (the short revolution) are tied to what is specifically a question of lifestyle in the United States.

In 1991, Juliet B. Schor published an influential book titled *The Overworked American: The Unexpected Decline of Leisure*,[11] in which she demonstrated that Americans then were working more and having less leisure time than they had before World War II. While her book provided a rich understanding of how the American standard of living reached a level of material comfort that far surpassed that of every other country, she explained how the desire to acquire goods and live in a consumer society in effect drove personal attitudes and values toward working more and having less free time.

Today, we live in a society in which children's playtimes are often scheduled as "playdates." We can use online services to buy almost anything, from gifts to groceries, from home or work. We can meet others, conduct romances, and live in a different life in a fantasy world via the Internet. We can shield ourselves from unwanted phone calls by blocking calls, using caller-ID, or letting voicemail answer for us. All of these examples give witness to Schor's predictions about the decline of leisure, but they also reflect a lifestyle that increasingly embraces the use of technology to give us greater control over our busy lives. Whether the pace of American life has accelerated as part of our more demanding consumer lifestyles or not, human beings naturally want to control their lives. As we work more, seek to gain status and consumer goods, and try to maintain the equilibrium necessary for survival in a busy world, why shouldn't we use the technologies that promise us greater control? The examples in this book provide a window on understanding the relationships among historical and contemporary forms of communication, social issues, and culture, and how they affect our lives.

CONTROLLING TIME AND SPACE

Though we don't often consciously dwell on how each new technology influences our sense of time and space, these issues have always formed a basis for understanding cultural change. Scholars have demonstrated how powerful these factors are in shaping social attitudes and values. Edison's invention of the electric light bulb was credited for changing how Americans approached activities that had formerly been structured because of available daylight. The electric light metaphorically turned night into day and brought about a culture that no longer was reliant on sunlight to provide a "productive" workday.

Lewis Mumford wrote about the impact of the clock on the fifteenth-century life of Benedictine monks, who began to regulate their prayers and daily activities in response to the bells in the clock tower.[12] Before long, other people within range of the bells also began to regulate their workday to the cues provided by the bells, and social life started to revolve around the clock and the characteristics of mechanical clock time.

The old-fashioned clock imposed arbitrary units to systematize time into sixty seconds that made up a minute, and sixty minutes in an hour. Controlling time began to influence the workday in stores, fields, and in other social organizations. As clocks became more commonplace, they regulated activities in communities and imposed a structure of thinking about time and life. During the industrial revolution, factory owners adopted the clock as the regulator of all human activity on the assembly line, and the concept that "time was money" dictated social relations in the factory. The psychologist Bernard Doray writes of the rules in the factory in 1863:

> Regulations specifying starting times, and the corresponding sanctions for late arrival, are an expression of the employers' attempts to impose a rigid working day; workers who were five minutes late were often fined, and in no case could they be more than fifteen minutes late without being fined. Repeated late arrival led to heavier fines and eventually to dismissal.[13]

During the industrial revolution, the factory assembly line became synonymous with scientific management and social control. These revolutions in using time as an agent of social change were much more gradual than today's rapid adoption of the cell phone, but the social phenomenon was similar. Doray describes how this social control alienated the workers. The point is, then, that when technologies influence time, humans have to adapt, either because the institutions in which they live become affected by time management or because the time characteristics of the technology with which they work get changed. And the individual is not immune to reacting psychologically to this type of control.

We are still slaves to clocks today, but our concept of time has changed because of the clocks we use. If you were to ask someone with a traditional analog watch what time it is, he or she might respond, "Oh, it's about quarter to one." Someone with a digital watch might answer, "It's 12:43 and 10 seconds." We have moved from the relatively "sloppy" sense of analog time to the precision of digital time. Analog time, with hands sweeping around a clock face, presented us with a sense of *synchronous* time, a visual representation of past, present, and future. The digital display presents *asynchronous* time, showing only the present moment, and therefore is decontextualized time[14]—that is, time that has no context to which we can relate. Not only does the appearance of the clock face influence how we "see" and experience time, but today time can be actualized by other technologies without our having to think about it at all. Now we have watches, clocks, and appliances that beep, tap us, flash, and even turn themselves on or off. Cell phones, computers, coffeemakers, thermostats, video recorders, automobiles, and garage doors, among other items, can be digitally programmed to run themselves or to monitor their own actions. When this happens, we cede a conscious awareness of the elements of time to the technology, or in other words, the technologies can appear to control us.

The anthropologist Edward T. Hall writes about the cultural implications of synchronous time and observes that synchronicity contributes to a feeling that we can only do one thing at a time.[15] By contrast, asynchronous time provided by a digital watch is nonlinear, essentially void of a sense of continuity. Digital time encourages us to think in fragments, with little connection to a sense of process. Is it any wonder, then, that younger people who have grown up knowing only digital technologies develop a sense of time that is less connected to a sense of history and look for quick answers rather than synthesizing different pools of information or engaging in complicated deliberation?

We can also see how the economy of time influences our behaviors. Mumford's writing on the impact of the clock shows how time becomes a commodity in the sense that it provides us with the means to structure our work and personal lives. But time is also a unit of measurement for using cell phones and the Internet. Use is measured in units computed by the second and millisecond—all easily measurable by digital technologies, and yet we often seem unaware that our charges are associated with our technology use. The companies that provide us with these services know that by selling us large "packages" of use time, they distract us from thinking about its cost—the way we might have in the "old" days, when a long-distance call racked up charges. Only when something goes terribly wrong, like the teenager with her first cell phone who goes well beyond the minutes of her packaged plan to rack up exorbitant charges, does the connection between technology use and money become obvious, and the "time equals money" equation becomes painfully clear.

Jeremy Rifkin begins chapter 1 of his book *Time Wars: The Primary Conflict in Human History* with these words: "It is ironic that in a culture so committed to saving time we feel increasingly deprived of the very thing we value."[16] We've come to regard speed, as represented by today's electronic technologies, as a desirable quality. The legacy of American efficiency and centralization—the idea that "bigger is better"—has given way to the belief that "faster is better."[17] And yet, technologies that work at a speed faster than our minds can comprehend distance our bodies and minds from the process of interaction. This can condition us to be impatient, rushed, and intolerant of any time we can't control.

If some technologies, such as the cell phone and Internet, give us the illusion of controlling time, they also offer the freedom of space—to move far beyond the confines of a wired phone, the traditional office, or the stacks in a library—and still have access to information and communication. Because they are wireless and instantaneous, they render irrelevant the question of where anyone or anything we are accessing may be physically located at that moment. But the term "space" has connotations beyond the obvious. Space can be both literal and figurative, and thinking about space helps us understand the impact of cell phones and the Internet. After all, if the Internet is the "information superhighway," the metaphor is transportation, and transportation suggests both time and space in the process of moving from point A to point B.

Space has yet another figurative connotation. Cyberspace is that ephemeral concept of space, that place, where we interact with computers over the Internet. Where is the information we seek? Where are those people who write to us, or to whom we write? Knowledge of physical location becomes unimportant to anyone who uses computers and the Internet. Yet there is still a sense of space on our computer monitors, one that sometimes competes with our daily relationship to the three-dimensional world.

Joshua Meyerowitz[18] has studied electronic technology and how it divorces us from traditional notions of space. He posits that electronic technology provides a sense of "placelessness" that is very much a part of a digital world because there is no concrete, physical sense of space. We don't observe or intuit where messages come from or where they go when we push the "send" button. To elaborate on his idea, we can think of how online "communities" are formed that are not physically located in a geographic vicinity, such as traditional communities in which we might know many people by name or face. In cyberspace, there is little knowledge of what the person you're e-mailing looks like, or, if you're in a chat room, how many lurkers (people who read messages but don't post any) might be watching, but not participating.

The time/space issue is at the heart of using cell phones and the Internet. While each is available twenty-four hours a day, seven days a week, the time features give the illusion of allowing us to control our lives, but the space issues reinforce all that is good about using cell phones and the Internet. We can easily see the benefits of working from home (unless the distractions of home are too great to get anything done), but we might not easily realize that our need to feel a part of a community, socially or professionally, is satisfied more by face-to-face communication with others rather by than by sitting alone at a computer, no matter where we are. At the same time, though, computers connected to the Internet and cell phones give people freedom to live in areas that might be more physically and economically suitable. Furthermore, the time and space manipulations lead us to think in different ways about what might have formerly been clear delineations between private and public behavior.

CHANGING BEHAVIORS AND ATTITUDES

Every once in a while, the proliferation of cell phones sets up a situation in which people look twice at the person using a cell phone. You don't normally expect people lounging in a park, sitting on a beach, or even dining in a restaurant, to be chatting away while relaxing or eating. And yet, we know when phones ring in inappropriate places or when people are talking in public places where you might not expect them to be on a phone, something in our culture seems to be changing. Perhaps the ability to make and receive a call anywhere, anytime, is part of the *technopoly* that Postman discusses. But at the same time, cell phones ringing and personal conversations in "inappropriate" places illustrate how time and space issues affect our social use of technology.

We often see how behaviors and attitudes are changing in our society when we look at what "other" people do. Sometimes the transition from *un*usual to usual just takes time and getting used to seeing others behave in ways we don't expect. But we seldom notice how we contribute to creating or accepting new behaviors in social settings.

Anyone who travels by air knows what happens in airports. Otherwise pleasant people seem to abandon their real selves and assume radically different behaviors in airports and on planes. Even though passing through long security lines has become routine, people seem to squirm, fidget, and sigh, while others take too long to load their computers, shoes, belts, and other paraphernalia into the plastic bins.

Then, when their turn comes, they too seem to move in slow motion, oblivious to the same stares, sighs, and frustration they themselves just demonstrated toward the people before them. Once in the designated waiting areas, they may converse on cell phones or tap away at their laptops. When the plane arrives, they rush to line up even before the boarding call has been made. When airline personnel attempt to seat passengers in an orderly manner by admitting those with seats in the back of the plane first, people still cluster as close as they can at the jetway door, even though their seats are reserved in the front of the plane. Once on the jetway, many continue to speak on their cell phones, and think that they have to speak louder because they're in a confined setting. Eyes roll as they wait for others to find their seats and stow personal items. Usually the ubiquitous cell phone stays in sight, with people talking as long as they possibly can before the flight attendant announces that all electronic devices have to be shut down before the plane takes off. Then, something remarkable happens. Someone, usually a few someones, seems afraid to turn his or her phone off and continues to speak, ignoring several requests to shut all electronics off. As soon as the plane touches down at the destination, the cell phones come out again. When the two arrival bells sound, the travelers leap to their feet to squeeze off the airplane, as though the experience was a painful ordeal. Then they rush down the jetway, through the halls, cell phones pressed against the sides of their heads. They sprint to the baggage claim section, where once again, they must wait, and they appear to be surprised that their luggage isn't there yet. With so many people traveling so much these days, wouldn't it be logical to think that this type of crowd mentality would be a rarity, rather than the norm? How often do we realize that we, too, get swept up in the airport frenzy and act just like those we criticize? How often do we allow ourselves to act like the other frustrated travelers, even when our purpose for traveling is to take a vacation or go somewhere to relax?

The reason, of course, is that it is much easier to criticize others than it is to criticize or even be aware of our own behaviors. For many people, appropriate behavior in one's private life doesn't always seem to translate well to public places. In a 2004 *New York Times* article, the journalist Ken Belson related the story of a woman who was flying on a US Airways flight from Miami to Philadelphia.[19] She refused the multiple requests by flight attendants to get her to shut down her phone so that the plane could take off, claiming that it would be rude to her caller if she did so. By the time the incident was over, the woman had slapped a federal air marshal, the plane was forced to return to the terminal, and the woman ultimately was taken away in handcuffs, charged with assault, and later prosecuted.

The woman in question might have been an otherwise wonderful person who had never broken the law and she may have truly believed that it would be rude to hang up on her caller, but what makes people feel that they are privileged to do what they want to do on a public air carrier, despite airline safety regulations and socially approved behavior? In his analysis of the situation, Belson describes how the woman's selfish behavior and the consequences of her actions created a stir among other passengers, who were justifiably upset about the public disturbance and the inconvenience. Even though other people on the plane tried to convince the woman that she was acting selfishly, she maintained her position that it would have been rude to terminate her phone call. Her moral justification for her position is what is known as the "actor-observer paradox," meaning that she couldn't see the consequences of her actions, though she might have been quick to point out what other people were doing that she deemed "wrong."

CULTURAL CHANGES

The more the pace of technological change accelerates, the more we need to consider the effect technology has on society. Understanding how technology influences social relations and cultural values and how it is changing our world becomes more important every day. In the realm of communication and media, these technologies and others have the power to transform lives—from ameliorating a sense of place or time, to structuring our days and controlling what we know about one another. Cell phones and the Internet have in their short histories brought about more changes to traditional behaviors, attitudes, and values than any other technologies or services in history. They do this because they are small, portable, fast, increasingly accessible, and relatively affordable.

This book draws attention to our everyday lives and how we've begun to use cell phones and the Internet in ways that point to a change in our culture. Our private lives are becoming less private, and our public lives are merging with our private lives. Our workdays can now be—and sometimes do approach—twenty-four hours long, and we tend to work seven days a week, even on vacations, if we take them. Even though we may think that cell phones and the Internet give us greater control over how we live our lives and how we use our time, we may find that we actually have more stress because we're expected to get things done faster, anywhere, anytime. We may actually spend less time with others in interpersonal communication and more time online or leaving messages. The changes that we see in others may cause us some concern, but our own behaviors and attitudes also become shaped by social factors that we tend to justify as morally acceptable for our own purposes.

The chapters in this book explore how and why our culture is changing by focusing on how cell phones and the Internet provide contexts for social change.

These two technologies are of particular importance because they have the ability to operate twenty-four hours a day, seven days a week, and they can free us from traditional ways of thinking that were circumscribed by norms of private and publicly acceptable behaviors, but at the same time, they offer portability and ubiquity but demand reaction and response. In the process, we need to consider whether we actually use them to improve communication, or merely, to substitute reaction for communication. In thinking about how, why, and what these technologies offer us, and how we make sense of using them on a daily basis, we can better understand how our society and culture are undergoing change, and we can speculate on new behaviors, attitudes, and values that will emerge in the future.

Two

A Cultural History of Cell Phones and the Internet

Although cell phones and the Internet may seem to be relatively new technologies, both trace their history to the development of wired forms of telegraph and telephone, and wireless radio. Each of these technologies played its own part in altering concepts of time and space and blurring the boundaries between public and private communication in American culture. This chapter discusses how our legacy communication technologies contributed to cultural changes that also influenced time, space, and public and private behaviors and demonstrates how cell phones and the Internet assumed some of the cultural baggage of previous communication technologies. The social impact of the earlier technologies undoubtedly contributes to what people think about cell phones and the Internet today and about their impact on culture.

Thinking about what contributes to a cultural history of any technology may appear at first to be an exercise more suited to the academic mind, but many people want to understand the world in which they live. Part of the fascination with everyday technology is that when people are part of a new experience—radio, television, the Internet, cell phones, or, maybe in the future, teleporting their bodies to another location—they know that change is in the air. They generally feel that there is something lost as well as something gained when these technologies become mainstream.

Entire generations become defined by the technologies they use. People are often circumspect when a new technology is introduced, especially when younger generations become the experts on its use. For the radio generation (anyone born before 1940), now referred to as the "Matures" by Karen Riggs[1] and others, their children, called the Baby Boomer TV generation, seemed to process information faster and more visually. For the TV generation, whose children grew up in homes with multiple cable channels, VCRs, home computers, the Internet, and video games, the pace of change has been even faster. The Boomers' kids, who became known as the "X" and "Y" generations, seemed much better at understanding digital technologies, working with computers, and figuring out digital logic. Now, the children of the "X" and "Y" generations seem to be able to program technology, manipulate content, and communicate digitally far more efficiently and capably than their parents. Each of these generations grew up in a slightly different communication and information environment, and each generation has defined its place in our common culture by using the technologies available to it in ways that astound older generations. Cultural histories examine the dynamics among technologies, people who use them, and the changes in our society that result from new social practices.

Some of the first serious academic studies of the impact of technology in the United States grew from what became known as the "Chicago School" of Sociology at the University of Chicago in the 1920s.[2] At that time, the city of Chicago was becoming a bustling city and major hub for railway traffic. The automobile had already changed where and how different economic classes could live and work, and public transportation was starting to become available for those who couldn't afford their own vehicles. The telephone facilitated business interactions, and women had entered the workforce as telephone operators, secretaries, and clerks.

The Chicago School introduced new methods of researching and evaluating social change. Over the years this interest in technology and society has been refined by disciplinary scholars and popular culture pundits to further understand how technology, social use of technologies and services, and cultural values respond to innovation, and how we, as individuals, adopt new tools and techniques in a socially constructed environment, such as workplace or home, or as a form of recreation or play. Courses examining the impact of technology in our society and around the world have grown in schools around the country in departments as diverse as English, history, anthropology, communication, American studies, and sociology. Part of the fascination with this topic might have to do with the fact that technologies are being invented and sold to the public very quickly these days. Many of us are acutely aware of how our own daily lives have embraced electronic technologies, and we seek to understand what has influenced our lives. Some may look to these topics as a guide to what areas of growth we can expect and what opportunities may be possible from the entrepreneurial perspective. A third possible reason is that many people are fascinated by images from science fiction that have now become reality. People live on a space station in outer space;

laser surgery seems to work miracles and speed the body's recovery; the Enterprise is no longer a film or television vehicle—it is the name of a space shuttle; even the Terminator was elected governor of California. Whatever the reasons for the growth of interest, and they are probably complex, studies to understand technology's form and function have become more popular than ever and have emerged from the academic world to influence popular culture and everyday thought.

Almost all studies of technology focus on aspects of innovation, how audiences use technology, or on the social relationships that occur when using technology. When examined together, it becomes possible to understand how contemporary needs, attitudes, and beliefs influence the adoption of a technology and how the technology finds utility according to the social conditions that influence its use. As Carolyn Marvin observes, "New practices do not so much flow directly from technologies that inspire them as they are improvised out of old practices that no longer work in new settings."[3]

Though innovation, or the invention of a new technology, seems like the logical place to begin to understand the impact of social change, it is really the least reliable factor to consider. Many technologies take many years to become successful, and if they succeed, it is usually because someone is able to demonstrate particular applications of those technologies that appeal to enough people to make them profitable. Many independent telephone companies were established in the early days, but they were soon purchased by the American Telephone and Telegraph Company (AT&T), which was granted a monopoly to provide telephone service in the United States in 1913. (AT&T was allowed to operate as a monopoly until 1983, at which time the government deregulated the telephone industry and opened it to competition from other telephone companies.) Technically, wireless telephony could have been available in the early part of the twentieth century,[4] but AT&T executives decided to keep telephony separate from experiments in radio. Even television was technically feasible as early as 1927,[5] but the image was poor and the cost of receivers too prohibitive for enough consumers to be interested in the few signals that were being transmitted.

Though there are some people who like to adopt the newest technologies, most are reticent to try them unless the services seem to be worth the expense. Even though cell phones were commercially introduced in 1985, cell phone companies didn't hit on the concept of selling cell phones for safety reasons until ten years later, when there were areas that had enough coverage to reasonably assure consumers that an emergency call could be answered. The Internet was operational in the 1960s, but didn't become a phenomenon until the early 1990s, when commercial enterprises started to offer a wider range of services that people could use in their homes and the cost of personal computers came down.

Time in history is the wild card in trying to understand how technologies change social relations. Probably no one could have predicted that communications could be shut down entirely when Hurricane Katrina hit communication networks in and around New Orleans and coastal Mississippi in 2005, affecting the ability of people to contact their families and friends, and for the government and journalists to get critical information to victims and to the rest of the public. The result of the devastation was the realization that the United States did not have an adequate wireless emergency network to aid in the disaster or its aftermath, and the event accelerated attempts to revise a communications plan for the area, to be used in the event of another potential disaster.

History does tend to repeat itself, and for that reason this chapter provides some background for how the technologies that eventually evolved into cell phones and the Internet began to shape the way we communicate today. All three components, invention, audience, and time in history, will help illuminate the ongoing story of the technological development of both cell phones and the Internet and of the services on which we've come to rely. What emerges is a picture of how the inventions, audiences, and social relations have come together to challenge us with new social environments that blur what has traditionally been viewed as private and public communication. When we project what we know has happened with these types of technologies in the past, we can make some educated guesses about the future and examine how these digital technologies have unique characteristics that influence social and cultural change.

COMMUNICATION TECHNOLOGY AND SOCIAL CHANGE

Ah, if only we could *accurately* predict the future! What a fortune we could make! How popular we might be! The problem is, of course, that predictions may be educated guesses, and no one can be sure of how and what lies ahead. Until an accurate crystal ball is invented, even the most careful predictions can only be guided by historical precedent, understanding how people begin to use new technologies and knowing how the use of technology changes over time. When it comes to cell phones and the Internet, it might be possible to say that both are 120-year overnight successes that originally grew from the environment that allowed wired communication—especially telegraph and telephone to form the first major phase of wired communication in the United States. The second major phase occurred in the mid-twentieth century with cable television and the Internet.[6] What can be traced, however, is the way people thought about the telegraph and telephone and how those technologies influenced social behavior, attitudes, and values. The following brief snapshots of social change explain how each of the legacy technologies made its own cultural impact. These examples encapsulate the essence and range of the power of the legacy technologies to create cultural change.

Telegraph

In 1881, *Scientific American* published a statement that telegraph would promote the "kinship of humanity."[7] As utopian as that thought was, many people who couldn't comprehend how this technology would work feared it and thought that the new wires strung across the country were the cause of the spread of cholera.[8] Other stories and legends told of how the telegraph aided in misinformation, such as when, in 1897, William Randolph Hearst dispatched Frederic Remington to illustrate the war in Cuba. On finding the area peaceful, Remington supposedly sent a telegram to Hearst asking for permission to return home. Hearst allegedly replied, "You furnish the pictures, and I'll furnish the war." And in a more humorous vein, but also foreshadowing the abbreviated language of a text message, a reporter once sent a telegram to Gary Grant's agent saying, "How old Cary Grant?" The actor supposedly replied, "Old Cary Grant fine. How you?"[9]

Though many inventors in several countries worked on developing a system of telegraphy that could communicate over distances using electrical wires, Samuel F. B. Morse is often credited as the "inventor" of the telegraph. What he did contribute to the effective use of telegraphy was an efficient language for sending messages over wires through a system of electronically generated dots and dashes. When Morse developed Morse code in 1844, the United States was still a country in formation. The population was scattered throughout the country, but the human migration westward was the most noticeable feature of the population drift. At that time, the dominant technological means of travel was the train, but time zones had not yet been coordinated throughout the growing United States. Each community had the right and the ability to determine the time within its own locality. When the final golden spike was driven into the earth uniting rails from the east and west, the United States had as many as 200 time zones. The train, however, knowing no restrictions by time zone, needed a better way to coordinate activities, deliver goods, pick up passengers, and deliver mail. By 1883, a system of coordinated time zones was established, making commerce and travel by rail a far more orderly process and giving the telegraph operator (a job often held by a man, even though women, too, were telegraph operators) a certain social status as an expert.[10]

The appearance of the electrical wires beside the train tracks was not immediately welcomed by those settlers who reveled in the open scenery of the West, in part because they were an unsightly mess, but also because they brought new ideas from the east to the west. News could be transmitted over the telegraph wires and published in local newspapers, and catalogs and new products from the east could be more easily transported by rail. The way of life that the pioneers forged began to change, and for the first time in the newly forming United States, information could unite the coasts, just as the railroad did. The vast expansion toward the west was becoming less of a distance, since information and transportation brought news, goods, and people to newly formed cities across the country. Time and space were being conquered by the emerging technology, and the telegraph played a major role.

Wired Telephone

In 1876, when Alexander Graham Bell patented and began to demonstrate his "harmonic telegraph," soon to be called the telephone, immigration from other countries and westward expansion were both under way. Most people still lived, worked, and died within ten miles of where they were born, but the United States was steeped in the industrial revolution, and railroads made it possible for types of industries to become established in specific locations.

Early predictions about the social impact of the telephone, like the telegraph, included their share of amusing anecdotes. Ithiel de Sola Poole[11] recounted how the telephone was predicted to eliminate regional dialects and have the effect of eliminating written records for historians, and allegedly Bell himself thought that the technology would be used to record voices so that family members would be able to remember loved ones after their death.

At first, telephones seemed strange and unnecessary, reinforcing the idea that innovation alone is not enough to create social change. Until individuals found a need for telephones, they remained an interesting novelty. In his book *America Calling: A Social History of the Telephone to 1940*, Claude S. Fischer discusses how telephone company salesmen attempted to cultivate different users. The first group to be targeted were businessmen, who were persuaded to use the telephone to be efficient, to save time, and to impress customers.[12] Later, when the residential market was targeted, the same claims to improve efficient running of the household were a large part of the phone company's efforts to entice women to use the telephone. Carolyn Marvin shows how the world of telephony quickly became commandeered by men who professed technological expertise and who considered women's conversation frivolous. Men viewed women's social communication as "gossip" and considered it a waste of time. "From a male perspective, the usual puzzles of communication between the sexes were exacerbated by technological codes that bound men but that women did not respect."[13] What became even more important was the number of new jobs that brought women from the privacy of the home into the public and to the office.

As the population shifted across the United States and cities became centers for business, women entered the workforce, often as telephone operators, secretaries, and clerks. It was assumed that the gentle, slightly higher timbre of the woman's voice would be heard more easily through the primitive coaxial copper cable, but the real reason women entered the office and clerical professions was that the increasing centralization of office activities allowed for greater specialization of the tasks within an office. Women became the equivalent of a paid office-wife, taking care of the man, who was too busy to be bothered by the mundane routine of keeping the office going. Once women began to earn their own livings, their social status began to change. The acceptance of women as workers outside the home changed dynamics in the home, and the rocky road toward gender equality had begun. John Brooks has summarized the number of changes very nicely:

What has the telephone done to us, or for us, in the hundred years of its existence? . . . It has saved lives by getting rapid word of illness, injury or famine from remote places. By joining with the elevator it has made possible—for better or worse—the multistory residence or office building. . . . Beyond a doubt it has crippled if not killed the ancient art of letter writing. It has made living alone possible for persons with normal social impulses; by so doing, it has played a role in one of the greatest social changes of this century, the breakup of the multigenerational household.[14]

By the middle of the twentieth century, so many social changes had occurred that the telephone had become one of the instrumental tools for modern society. Along with changes in transportation, home entertainment, urban development and changes in labor, industry, and the family, telephones had gone from being a luxury to being considered a necessity for businesses and in the home. Phone books were published to list the names, numbers, and addresses of telephone subscribers, and seeing one's name in print was not only a measure of status, but of pride. As the number of phone calls increased and telemarketers began to target homes, the use of the telephone for anything other than social speech or work began to raise questions of personal privacy. As more people requested their names be deleted from telephone books, publishers of the phone directories realized that there would be more money to be made by charging customers to have an unlisted number than to list them.

Other technologies were also developed to help keep peace in the home and to increase efficiency in the office. Telephone answering machines, which had been around in a primitive form since the late 1930s, became fully functional for home and business uses in the late 1970s. Caller ID, voice mail, and other services began to be marketed to home users for purposes of controlling privacy. Businesses adopted these services, in part, to be responsive to callers, but also to avoid having to retain more employees to constantly cover outside calls. James Katz provides a far more thorough analysis of the impact of attempts to control privacy with additional telephone technologies in his book *Connections*.[15] By 2001, the explosion of telemarketing had become such a big business that many citizens began to ask the government for protection from unwanted and annoying calls. In July 2003, the Federal Trade Commission (FTC) created a Do Not Call Registry that people could sign for, and it effectively prohibited commercial telephone solicitations to those people. Over 50 million people signed up by October 1, and new registrations continue.

The impact of the deregulation of AT&T and the subsequent divestiture of the Bell Operating Companies in 1984[16] allowed for a flurry of competition in the telephone industry in the United States. While many companies mounted battles for subscribers and enhanced services, others looked toward the convergence of wired and wireless forms to capitalize on the technical developments that led to using more of the electromagnetic spectrum for wireless communications, and cell phone services began to receive more attention.

The Growth of the Cell Phone

Like many contemporary technologies, the cell phone also had a long history before it was commercially introduced in 1984. Various manufacturers and electronics companies attempted to develop portable, wireless telephones, but until Bell Labs effectively began to use a segment of the electromagnetic spectrum for efficiency by dividing the frequencies into "cells," in 1947, wireless phones remained limited to special purposes and operated at relatively high cost. Cell phones are a result of the convergence of the telephone and the radio. The cellular telephone unit has a low-power radio transmitter that is extremely sophisticated and can sense where the caller is, in relation to the closest transmitter. The term "cell" refers to an area of coverage, usually about 10 square miles. When you move about with a cell phone, the transmitter in the phone senses when you are coming to the end of the "cell" and automatically shifts you into the next cell for continuous coverage. Obviously, the more often there are high-quality towers in the area, the better the coverage. When the phone is "roaming," it is searching for the nearest tower to retransmit its signal.

First-generation cell phones were analog based and limited to voiced communication that could be connected to wired forms. Initially, cell phones mounted in cars seemed to be the likely method of creating more mobile communication, but relatively few consumers seemed interested in car phones, because they were awkward and expensive and seemed to be a target for thieves. Motorola was one company that took the lead in developing the U.S. market and invested close to $100 million in the development of the cell phone between the late 1960s and the early 1980s. Even then, by 1983, when the first Motorola phone was made available, it weighed about two pounds.[17]

Second-generation cell phones used digital waves, and the smaller, digital signals allowed for greater sharing of frequencies. The second-generation phones offered expanded capabilities that could enable phones with text features, camera functions, and audio and video downloading. Finally, as the cost of calling packages came down, the range of services began to grow, and cell phone towers extended the range of making calls, cell phones finally caught on throughout the United States.

Although the difference between the first-and second-generation cell phones was extraordinary, the difference between second- and third-generation (3G) phones extends even further. In countries where wired telephony has not been as available as in the United States, 3G phones have created a rapid cultural change in communication in and among the people. In many of those societies, the cultural changes are far more drastic than in the United States (some examples will be discussed in later chapters).

As is obvious from the very basic description above, geographic areas that have little or no natural or human-made barriers probably receive the most reliable, high-quality cell phone services, especially within one cell. In a country the size of the United States, where the population is distributed over millions of square miles, the uneven number of cell towers may result in areas of no service or areas that have more signal interference, resulting in call quality that is not as good as the traditional wired phone. As cell phones become more sophisticated and consumers begin to use 3G cell phones in the United States, the range of possible uses continues to grow. In one small handheld device, it is already possible to handle financial transactions, download music and movies, take pictures, and handle simple computational processes. Could the cell phone transform the need for personal computers? Technologically it could; but how long might that take before it becomes the preferred use for accessing the Internet?

The Growth of the Internet

While the history of the innovation of the cell phone is more closely allied to the companies and corporations that were already working in wired telephony and other communications technologies and less to individuals whose personalities influenced the development of the technology, the evolution and growth of the Internet is more closely aligned to the insights and applications of individuals who have become celebrities and folk heroes in the growth of this medium. Names such as Grace Murray Hopper, Joseph C. R. Licklider, Vint Cerf, and Tim Berners-Lee and acronyms such as MIT (the Massachusetts Institute of Technology), ARPANET (Advanced Research Projects Agency-Network), and CERN (translation, the European Organization for Nuclear Research) are a part of the history of the innovation of the Internet and the World Wide Web.[18]

Though reducing the various innovations to a few simple paragraphs for a snapshot of the innovations that contributed to the development of the Internet can in no way do justice to the complex evolution of this global phenomenon, some attention can be focused on the critical developments that brought the Internet to the attention and use of businesses and home users. From the beginning, Licklider, Cerf, and Berners-Lee were interested in developing a wired system of communication that would allow multiple users to share a network, and they used the resources of their organizations to integrate concepts and technologies for experimentation and implementation.

Although innovations leading toward the development of packet switching, computer development, and wired and wireless communications were taking place in a number of countries in the 1960s, the U.S. Department of Defense's Advanced Research Projects Agency (ARPA) funded a project that would focus on creating systems to allow computers to interact. Over the following two decades, there were many advances made in computers, protocols, and computer languages, which were developed by researchers at MIT and other institutions, and by young people working on these projects at home. The extraordinary success of Bill Gates and Steve Jobs in developing affordable computers with user-friendly features for the average consumer elevated each of these young men to cult heroes and made them very rich computer tycoons. In summarizing the collective vision of the entrepreneurs in computer and Internet history, Howard Reingold writes,

> The essential elements of what became the Net were created by people who believed in, wanted, and therefore invented ways of using computers to amplify human thinking and communication. And many of them wanted to provide it to as many people as possible, at the lowest possible cost. Driven

by the excitement of creating their own special subculture below the crust of the mass-media mainstream, they worked with what was at hand. Again and again, the most important parts of the Net piggybacked on technologies that were created for very different purposes.[19]

The entrepreneurs shared the goal of trying to create a system of communication that would be open to multiple users, and to make these technologies available to as many people as possible. What they proposed was a system that was built on trust and the belief that people would not abuse the networks or invade other computers. With the advent of Web 2.0, the Internet became a medium for which individuals could upload information just as easily as they could download it from various data banks, and the Internet then became a target, too, for people who wanted to become "electronic publishers" of information, as well as those who sought to exploit the interactive features of the medium by spamming, phishing, and other nefarious deeds that exploited the platform originally built on trust. While the innovations leading toward the Internet are many, Sara Kiesler has summed up the real impact of the Internet for daily life: "What makes the Internet special is not the technology per se, but the social interactions it is inspiring."[20]

With so many developments taking place at research universities around the United States, the development of computers fostered a subculture of computer students who became known as "hackers." In *The Second Self: Computers and the Human Spirit*, the psychologist Sherry Turkle writes about the emergence of hackers at MIT and the values and attitudes they held.[21] Her characterization of these students shows how attention and interest in the emerging field of computer science became not only an object of study, but also a way of life. In her description, she accurately identifies characteristics of a particular subgroup that has become synonymous with using computers and the Internet, and that introduced a number of attitudes, behaviors, and values we now see shared by many in the general population.

According to Turkle, the hacker subculture venerates individuality and sets itself apart from the rest of society. Individualism is key, even though social identity with other members of the subculture remains important to the expression of what being a hacker is all about. The hackers she describes developed their own jargon that set them apart from others, chose to work late into the evening and to interact more with the computers than with other human beings, and took great pride in their mastery over machines. What Turkle very eloquently characterizes is how a group of students felt superior to others when they mastered a technology system and felt they were "outlaws" by initiating viruses, worms, or other programs that could disrupt other computer users' lives. Their attitudes toward time in particular show a distain for traditional notions of when to work and when to sleep. Part of what they crave is mastery over cyberspace. And for the hacker, there is no such thing as private information when one can control someone else's information. While hackers may exhibit extreme attitudinal and behavioral traits, they also teach us a lesson about how the computer as a tool and how the Internet can become an all-encompassing world. Perhaps no one understands what "thinking digitally" means more than hackers, and they are masters at understanding the asynchronicity of computer interaction (I will further discuss this concept in following chapters). Technological superiority and the exercise of personal control are defining features of many of today's typical, computer-literate members of society, and allegiance to projects rather than to groups of people is a characteristic of their Internet expertise.

Hackers are an example of a group of people who understand the power of computers and the Internet to manipulate time and space, and they demonstrate extreme attitudes about what is private, as well as what they feel should be public knowledge or information. From a cultural perspective, hackers might be the extreme in terms of the audience that understands and can best manipulate the Internet, but hackers' attitudes, behaviors, and values are becoming more prevalent in society and the way they approach social interaction and problem solving shows how much computer and Internet expertise introduces new values to our culture.

Radio and Wireless Technologies

As we look toward a future in which different people with different levels of technical competence increasingly use cell phones and the Internet for a variety of purposes, it is useful to think of how and why cell phones and the Internet are increasingly becoming interoperable. This contributes to what *PC Magazine* referred to as the "New Mobile Revolution."[22]

When people hear the word "radio," they usually conjure an image of news, music, or talk in a broadcast form. The history of this medium and how it has been used is far more extensive and complex than even the history of the development of the Internet.[23] The term really encompasses both *radio* as broadcast communication form, and the *radio industry*, which suggests local and national programming. Broadcast radio even relied on wires to share information. From the very early days of radio broadcasting, remote pickups of news and coverage of political broadcasts or sporting events were sent to radio stations over telegraph or telephone wires. By 1922, stations became linked over phone lines for certain broadcasts, and by 1923, the first cable was laid to allow for permanent connections between two stations.[24] As the technology of radio diffused throughout the United

States, especially with the help of stations that were linked together forming networks for the purpose of sharing content, radio programs became so popular that families would gather in their living rooms to listen to nationally distributed programs. The popularity of many of those programs delivered to the American home, coast to coast, often set a national agenda for conversation about the topics and celebrities. Needless to say, the infrastructure of radio networking was well in place when television became the defining medium of the late twentieth century, and the same system of sharing programs from station to station through a system of wired and wireless technologies (especially when cable television became possible in the 1970s) has fueled American popular culture for decades.

The cultural impact of the radio and television industries and their role in American society is certainly worthy of study, but the cultural impact of cell phones and the Internet is a better example of how the Federal Communications Commission (FCC) has handled allocations of frequencies for nonfederal, unlicensed, personal, and commercial use. All wireless communication uses a part of the electromagnetic spectrum, which is the part of the atmosphere used for distributing radio frequencies, commonly called "airwaves." In 1934, when the FCC was formed, it was given the task of regulating the spectrum for the public's good. The airwaves were considered a public trust, and the FCC followed the precedents of its forerunner, the Federal Radio Commission (FRC), which had worked out a system of licensing broadcasters through the Department of Commerce.

By 1989, innovations in personal communication services (PCS) such as home or workplace wireless systems and the use of digital technologies had shown that the spectrum could be managed far more efficiently. The FCC began auctioning frequencies for personal uses in 1994 in addition to those it reserved for mobile communications, and allowed a number of small-format wireless technologies to be sold to business and home consumers. Now connections to the Internet can be made from several terminals through one router to WiFi systems in municipal locations, public buildings, stores, and coffee shops.

Using these frequencies, cell phones can handle more than voice communications. They can use text message features and can receive and send video files and music. BlackBerry and Treo may be the brand names most Americans know, but other multiuse devices generically called *smart phones* are constantly adding features that appeal to some consumers. As the cost of some of these phones come down over time and the number of features they offer continue to improve, it will be interesting to see how they compete for traditional cell phone customers.

Another distribution form that has potential to change the cost structure of sending material through wired and wireless technologies is the Voice over Internet Protocol, or VoIP. While the origin of VoIP can be traced to the early days of the

Internet, when in the United States it was referred to as "Voice Funnel" as part of an ARPA project involving packetized audio, it did not become a reliable method of voiced communications until 1995, when digital-signal processing (DSP) and microprocessors became sophisticated enough for mainstream use. Generically referred to as IP (Internet protocol) telephony, the first-generation technology required that users log on to the Internet to access other phoneware users through a directory service. Public directories or e-mail addresses routed calls to other IP telephone users. Each party had a microphone connected to a sound card in the computer; the phone software would then digitize and compress the audio signal and route it through connections over the Internet, where it would be modulated to an audio sound at the other end. In the early days, the modem speed often had to be adjusted for particular speech styles. Silence, for example, would send the modem into a "search" mode for frequency; once the new frequency was found, the levels had to be rebalanced. Once higher-speed modems began to be used, many of the problems inherent in voiced communication were corrected electronically. Since that time, a number of hardware and software vendors have emerged to improve various VoIP components. And although the sound quality has improved, some of the commercial VoIP providers have yet to be totally successful with connecting their VoIP users with conventional telephones, though progress toward this end is rapidly taking place. When this is effectively accomplished, the potential for the new global village will expand dramatically because, as David Greenblatt writes, "VoIP will change peoples' lives through increasingly personalized services."[25] The great benefit of VoIP is that it costs significantly less than traditional phone calls, and distance no longer seems to be a cost-prohibitive feature for telephone service. For example, in 2001, even though VoIP technology was not as widely available as it is today, on Mother's Day, ITXC, a VoIP carrier, announced that callers in the United States used 5.7 million minutes on its networks. In Mexico on the same day, over 4.2 million minutes were used. And in the United States, 96 percent of the calls made on that day were international calls, sent to over 200 countries.

In short, VoIP routes voice, data, and text over the Internet of any other IP-based network, rather than over traditional circuit-switched voice transmission lines. The flexibility afforded by VoIP architecture makes VoIP an exciting possibility for low-cost connections worldwide. In addition to facilitating communication among broadband (wired or wireless) and handheld devices, such as those used for a mobile phone, VoIP drives the convergence of other technologies and can be used for a number of value-added services, including speech recognition and virtual private networks. The system is reliable and interoperable, or able to operate over a variety of different platforms and networks in a seamless manner. The growth of mobile phones, particularly 3G phones, provides the necessary hardware for user-friendly services that thrive on VoIP.

INNOVATION, AUDIENCE, AND TIME IN HISTORY

Once audiences began to find uses for the innovations discussed in this chapter, new opportunities for social change became possible. From the westward expansion facilitated by the telegraph to the creation of cities and changes in gender relations in homes and businesses with telephones, to the subcultures of the Internet and the newest convergence of wired and wireless technologies, technologies have contributed to cultural changes at a specific time in history. Telegraph, telephone, and radio all served to unite people over distances and, over a 150-year period of history, became part of American life. All of these technologies also contributed to a sense of time and space and influenced the type of behaviors, attitudes, and values that were tied to public and private places. They aided in the settlement of the West, in the distribution of the population across the continental United States, and in the formation of new jobs, gender relations, and changes in the American family. As radio developed into a medium for the masses and the networking structure of the radio industry served as the basis for the emerging television industry, linking coasts through systems of wired and wireless technologies resulted in a national culture. These forms of mass media and media content that delivered similar ideas to national audiences united the country and defined what it meant to be American. The cultural themes, advertised products, ideas of what was important, news, and sense of how America viewed the world (and vice versa) became synonymous with progress, technology, and a sense of identity. The innovations and audiences that embraced them formed a communication infrastructure and a system that influenced social organization. To every generation born, the legacy of the way people used communication technologies defined what they knew and how they knew it.

Three

The Haves, Have-Nots, and Don't Wants

When *Time* magazine announced that the person of the year for 2006 was "You," the editors characterized their decision on the basis that "this was the year the people took control of the media. You changed the way we see ourselves, and the world we live in, forever."[1] Who was the "you" to whom *Time* magazine referred? How many "yous" made up the media revolution that the editors described? Even more importantly, who really has been affected by this revolution, and what impact will it have on our culture? The answers, in part, depend on who actually uses digital technology and who does not.

While communication technology before 1960 was primarily analog based, meaning that the signal used to transmit information came in analog waves, the communication technologies that we now have operate in digital modes. This shift from one fundamental electrical transmission form enables our "one-way" mass media forms of contemporary communication technologies to become "two-way" media and makes them capable of connecting to the Internet. As the American public negotiates using cell phones and the Internet for a greater number of purposes, the intersection of the technologies and the users' old habits, attitudes, and biases influence the way people adopt, embrace, or reject new technologies.

The term "digital divide" describes the concept that not everyone has equal opportunity to use digital technology. It generally refers to groups of people who are unable to participate in using computers or other digital technologies because of socioeconomic reasons that prevent them from getting *access* to hardware or to information. The concept is often translated into common discourse that defines the "haves" and the "have-nots." Typically, "have-nots" have been relegated to their position by either their own socioeconomic status or by lack of infrastructure to accommodate their needs, even if they can afford them. But today, access to some of these technologies goes beyond the matter affordability; the digital divide also can describe the gulf between people who choose to use them and who choose not to use them. While for many people, cell phones and the Internet have become necessities, but some people make conscious choices not to use them. We can call these people the "don't wants." These people are not necessarily curmudgeons, nor are they Luddites. Many have thoughtfully considered the impact of technologies and have strong reasons against using them, including cost, amount of time it takes to learn to use them, or lifestyle that doesn't require them. Others realize that these technologies have the potential to change their lives. In articulating his reason for why he doesn't want a cell phone, the *Newsweek* columnist Robert J. Samuelson spoke for many when he wrote,

> Someday soon, I may be the last man in America without a cell phone. To those who see cell phones as progress, I say: they aggravate noise pollution and threaten our solitude. The central idea of cell phones is that you should be connected to almost everyone and everything at all times. The trouble is that cell phones assault your peace of mind no matter what you do. If you turn them off, why have one? You just irritate anyone who might call. If they're on and no one calls, you're irrelevant, unloved or both. If everyone calls, you're a basket case.[2]

The framework of the haves, have-nots, and don't wants can be applied to understanding what people do with technology or how they cope without it. The features that many people do use are indicators of the type of social change that will be discussed in later chapters. And while there may be a general perception that "everybody" has cell phones and the Internet, the truth may lie closer to what the science fiction author William Gibson observed when he said, "The future is already here, it's just unevenly distributed."[3]

GENERALIZING THE "HAVES"

As previously mentioned, every generation seems to have a particular communication technology that helps define their worldview and their way of communicating. Marketers know that generally people within similar age groups have different lifestyle needs and pressures and that if any innovation is going to be successful, it will be because an audience begins to experiment with it, and use it. Audience use determines what other products, services, or commercial activities might evolve over time to continually drive interest and create more consumer demand.

Looking at age groups to understand culturally preconceived ideas about technology is one way of identifying who might use technologies, and for what purposes. The characteristics that different groups bring to the experience of using technology, whether by virtue of their age range or their classifications as niche audiences, relates to the content and access issues of using the Internet services and relying on cell phones. Niche audiences tell us much more about what appeals to certain groups and how people make sense of these technologies and services in their lives. As a result, looking at how people among niche audiences use technologies and services in their lives gives us a much better sense of how values, attitudes, and behaviors are shaped. Peer groups, socioeconomic similarities, and the institutions that most affect any group of individuals are mediating factors in forming peoples' attitudes, behaviors, and values toward technology use and social life. Perhaps, most importantly, the children of each generation define themselves *in contrast* to the attitudes, beliefs, and values of their parents. Whether this happens because of "rebellious youth" or in part because of the importance of peer pressure and defining one's self in relationship to one's family and society, each age group ends up using technology in their own ways.

A convenient way of making sense of the different age groups who use the Internet and the characteristics those groups share is to consider the descriptions of various generations, often seen in the popular press. In an effort to find a nonpejorative term for our culture's oldest segment, Americans have moved from describing this group as the elders, or elderly, to seniors. The term *Matures* now identifies the over-65 age group. Many of the members of this group fought in or lived through the experience of World War II (WWII) or Korea. Most remember growing up with newspapers and radio as the dominant media for news and entertainment. Some of the older members of this group may have experienced the Depression or come from families who maintained values that related to that period in history,[4] including a belief that social security would take care of them in their old age. Many believed that if they worked hard during their most productive years, they could take advantage of the standard retirement age of 65. A guaranteed social security income promised a life of leisure in their "golden years." What hadn't been considered adequately was the need that this group would have for affordable health care and medical facilities that could accommodate a population that was living longer.

The children of the Matures, the Baby Boomers (or Boomers), acquired their name as a result of having been born after WWII. In those years between 1946 and 1964, more babies were born than in any previous era in U.S. history. With more children to be educated, more schools were built, where students were encouraged to work hard so they could take advantage of the professional jobs that were a hallmark of the new service work that electronic technology provided. They also had the good fortune to live in the United States at a time when the economy was strong, and for many, college became another institution in which specialization and professionalism was promised along with a diploma. Opportunity and hard work seemed to characterize the Boomer desire to "have it all," and many characterized themselves as "workaholics." The Boomers also experienced the first big growth in consumer electronics and media that became oriented specifically to them. They comprised the first "television generation" and grew up with this form of media in the home. The development of the transistor made radio portable, and the FCC approval of FM radio transmissions in 1967 resulted in album-oriented rock, which became the representative musical form for the Boomers. Popular media shaped and reinforced their values. They rebelled against their parents and formed their social and political attitudes in the presence of Woodstock, Vietnam, Watergate, women's equality, and civil rights.[5]

The next generation came to be called "Generation X,"[6] the first generation born to Baby Boomers in the late 1970s and early1980s, and by contrast, they became characterized as "slackers." Perhaps because they saw their parents working so much, or having little time to spend with their children, many members of this generation chose to engage in less strenuous (or little) work and spend more time in pursuit of leisure. It could also be, perhaps, that this generation experienced the first wave of the video games, digital technologies such as CDs and DVDs, and the Internet. In fact, many of the architects of the Internet came from this group, as they began to unravel the mystery of digital technologies and think "outside the box" of mainstream mass mediated culture.

Shortly after Gen X came Generation Y, probably called so because there was little to differentiate them from the X's who preceded them, except that they were born into a world where digital technologies were beginning to appear at home, at work, and in schools. These children, born in to the later Boomers in the late 1980s, entered college around the turn of the century (the twenty-first century) and are also known as the Millennials. This generation never knew a time when there was no MTV, probably expected to go to college, and came from home environments where they had been constantly supervised throughout their early years. This group was in the first vanguard of cell phone and MP3 technology users who embraced downloading music and using the peer-to-peer file sharing characteristics of computers.

Today's teens have been dubbed "Generation C," with the "C" referring to content.[7] The defining technology for this group *is* the Internet. What sets this generation apart is a comfort and ease with digital content that allows them to create, generate, and post their own media content on the Internet. They have a very different attitude toward privacy, issues of copyright and ownership of media content, and publicizing their personal thoughts. More than any other group, this one has inculcated the changes in attitudes, beliefs, and values that cell phones and the Internet have made available to everyone.

Cell Phone Use and the American Public

As the categories of generations demonstrates, the communication technologies that are available to people define their lives and reflect their values. What becomes a cult classic or a children's' story, or even what type of adult themes appear in the media addresses audiences of different demographics, such as age, socioeconomic status, and gender. Those content issues reflect ideas that characterize peer groups and provide a common background that often marks a generation. They also influence what type of media content appeals to those groups as new media distribution forms, such as the Internet and cell phones, begin to be used for a wider range of services.

The cell phone study represented in Table 3.1 demonstrates how people have changed their behaviors to reallocate time and how this raises expectations of how available other people should be—all characteristics of the immediacy of digital communication forms. The study also calls attention to how people often use their cell phones to fill available time and indicates how communication patterns are changing.

As Table 3.1 indicates, cell phones users of different age groups tend to use their cell phones for different purposes. Across all age groups, the most common reason for people to have cell phones is for safety, and the results of the Pew Internet and American Life Project's study of cell phone users of different age cohorts shows that a significant number of cell users have used their phones in emergency circumstances.

Overwhelmingly, younger users, those of Generation C and Generation Y, tend to personalize their phones to a greater extent, fill free time while doing something else, and are surprised at the size of their monthly cell phone bills. Across the chart, the percentage of respondents who agree with the survey statements trails off as the cohorts age, with two slight exceptions: 10 percent of the Matures, aged over 65 years (compared with 9% of the 50–64 Boomer age group), claim that they are not always truthful about where they are when they're on their cell phones (leading to some interesting speculation as to what the Matures may be doing—perhaps when speaking to their own children). Additionally, the over-65 group also feels

Table 3.1
Cell Phone Users By Age

Experiences and attitudes	Percentage of cell phone owners in each age cohort who say				
	Ages 18–29	Ages 30–49	Ages 50–64	Age 65+	Total
Personalized their cells by changing wallpaper or adding ring tones	85%	72%	50%	29%	65%
I have used my cell phone in an emergency and it really helped	79%	76%	70%	65%	74%
I often make cell phone calls to fill up my free time while I'm traveling or waiting for someone	61%	43%	25%	20%	41%
I have occasionally been shocked at the size of my monthly cell phone bill	47%	38%	26%	23%	36%
When I'm on my cell phone I'm not always truthful about exactly where I am	39%	23%	9%	10%	22%
Too many people try to get in touch with me because they know I have a cell phone	37%	23%	12%	5%	22%
I often feel like I have to answer my cell phone even when it interrupts a meeting or a meal	31%	26%	14%	20%	24%
Received unsolicited commercial text messages	28%	15%	15%	13%	18%
I have drawn criticism or dirty looks because of the way I used my cell in public	14%	9%	4%	3%	8%
Used cell to vote in a contest shown on TV such as "American Idol"	14%	9%	5%	1%	8%

Source: Lee Rainie and Scott Keeter, "Cell Phone Use," Pew Internet & American Life Project, April 2006, http:www.pewinternet.org/pdfs/PIP_Cell_phone_study.pdf, 6. (accessed May 11, 2006). Based on an AOL cell phone survey conducted by Pew Internet & American Life Project, Associated Press, March 8–28, 2006. $N = 1.503$ (752 contacted on land lines and 751 contacted on their cell phones). In all, 1,286 cell users are in the sample. The margin of error for the cell-using population is ±3%. Used with permission.

compelled to answer the phone when it rings during a meal or meeting more than the 50- to 64-year-old age group (20% of the Matures compared with 14% of the Boomers), a feature that either reflects that the Matures' telephone habits predate answering machines or reflects that they may not have had these types of call blocking services.

In general, the study clearly shows that of those surveyed, younger cell phone users engage in a wider range of cell phone activities than older users and have become more devoted users. With the number of cell phones in America reaching 180.5 million by the end of 2005,[8] or approximately two-thirds of the nation, the cell phone has achieved critical mass.

Cell Phone Time and Space Matters

The term "smart mobbing" is used to describe how people pass along information in a spontaneous manner[9] and reflects how callers think about time from the perspective of wanting to share things immediately and fill slow moments. What the study does not investigate is whether people feel that their cell phone interactions are as rewarding as face-to-face communication or other forms of exchanging information.

Text messaging is an excellent example of how the cell phone can be used to manipulate time and space while changing the quality of interaction. Since cell phones are small and unobtrusive, they can be used inconspicuously. Because text messaging is silent, there are no social norms or taboos that call attention to the users in public places. Furthermore, the emerging language of text messaging saves the user time in composition, and the message can be stored just the same way that voice messages can be left for someone who has their cell phone in the "off" position, or who may be on another call. Table 3.2 identifies some of the common text messaging short cuts. The "language" of abbreviations is a time-saver, but it also demonstrates how young people often become the leaders in introducing new social practices through their use of technology, how they structure it for their own social needs, and, in the case of the C generation, how they create content that is appropriate to their needs, as well as how the technology communicates.

Text messaging also reflects both the way an age group adopts a technology and the way the group exerts a level of expertise over the technology. When you text message with a cell phone, you need to push many alphanumeric keys in succession. If you were to type the word "how," you would need to tap the number 4 key (with letters "ghi") twice, the number 6 key (with letters "mno") three times, and the number 9 (with letters "wxyz") once, to spell the word. This is

Table 3.2
New Languages

For text messaging			For instant messaging	
!-(	Black eye	BRB	Be Right Back	
!-)	Proud of black eye	JK	Just Kidding	
#-)	Partied all night	LOL	Laughing Out Loud	
#:-o	Shocked	LYLAS	Love You Like a Sister	
%*}	Inebriated	NP	No Problem	
%+{	Got beat up	OMG	Oh My God	
%-6	Brain-dead	POS	Parent Over Shoulder	
%-\	Hung over	ROFL	Rolling on Floor Laughing	
%-|	Worked all night	TTYL	Talk to You Later	
%\	Hangover	YW	You're Welcome	
>>:-	Furious			
<<				

Source: Lee Rainie, "Life Online: The Growth and Impact of the Internet (and Related Technologies)," Pew Internet & American Life Project, /CTCNet Conference, Washington, D.C., July 28, 2006, http://www.pewinternet.org//ppt//2006%20-%207.28.06%20CTNet%20–%final.pdf,9 (accessed November 12, 2006). Used with permission.

time consuming until one learns how to navigate the key pad efficiently, and many older cell phone users, particularly those with less than perfect eyesight or less than flexible thumbs, find this feature too time consuming and cumbersome. With the exception of PDA users and those who have cell phones with complete keyboards, text messaging tends to be a mode of communication favored by Generations C and Y. Of course, the ability to send these types of messages while other things are going on, like during school lectures, or in business meetings, makes the personal nature of sending messages in a space that would not accommodate verbal communication a potentially desirable alternative.

While texting might occupy someone while something else is going on, it also raises the question of whether people can effectively split their attention between competing forces. Many people use cell phones for voice or text without giving full attention to the message or whatever else might be going on—a particularly troublesome issue when using cell phones and driving are combined. Texting also demonstrates how younger cell phone users introduce new concepts to older users. The fastest-growing segment of the population who are learning how to text message are those parents who want to keep in touch with their children, especially when the children are away at school. A particularly pithy illustration of this was reflected in a *Boston Globe* article on the number of parents learning how to text, and cited research that claimed text messaging for the 45 through 65 age group had increased seven times faster than for the under-18 group in the period between September 2005 and September 2006.[10] As one parent reported, "You know, if I had asked her at dinner, 'How was school today?' she'd say 'Fine.' This gives her a way to talk to me without having to talk to me." For those of us interested in the nature of interaction, the lack of emotion signals an unhealthy sign for the quality of communication, and the question arises whether a response is the same thing as an interaction, but for a parent looking for some sign of acknowledgment from a daughter or son, the brief response may be important, and better than no response at all.

One potentially humorous example of how Generation C has learned to use cell phone features that can possibly annoy or embarrass older people who have lost the capability of hearing the high-pitched frequency is the *Mosquito*, a ringtone that emits a sound that young ears can hear, but that older ears may miss.[11] Students in a classroom are often amused by ringtones that the teacher can't hear, and this reinforces the rebellious nature of making the cell phone part of a generational artifact, as well as a subtle act of harmless rebellion.

Public and Private Matters

Often, the first thing many people mention when the subject of cell phones is raised is the annoyance of ringing phones in inappropriate places or someone talking loudly about personal matters. This type of unavoidable eavesdropping makes many people uncomfortable, and many public buildings and establishments have signs reminding owners to turn off their cell phones or to refrain from using them when they could interrupt someone else. The Pew Internet and American Life cell phone use study reflects relatively low scores for people who claim that they "have drawn criticism or dirty looks because of the way they use their cell phones in public," but these respondents might possibly be unaware of the looks they receive when they use their phones too, since individuals often feel morally superior to others when there is activity deemed inappropriate. Or, it is possible that using cell phones in public places is now being accepted more widely than before, and that others don't exhibit the same level of annoyance as in the earlier days of cell use. The third possibility is that cell users might be learning those appropriate behaviors about how and when to use their cell phones, and therefore they are not behaving as loudly or in inappropriate places. Whatever the real answer, this feature of using private communication forms in public places is often the cause for complaints.

However, everyone who has a cell phone knows that when a cell phone rings in a public place, a number of people start searching for their phones, hoping to respond before someone else gives them the "look"—the head turn, the disgusted scowl, or sometimes the grunt, that non-cell phone users give to those whose phones ring in public places. Even if the ringtone isn't your own, it's hard not to want to appear responsive, so people often clamor to find their phones and answer them, or at least, put them in silent mode. This has resulted in a new social malady called "cell phone anxiety," and while the behavior may appear Pavlovian, many cell phone users report that they do feel bad when they forget to turn their cell phones off in some social settings where disturbances are readily acknowledged as inappropriate.

The survey data that ask whether people have taken steps to personalize their phones show how individuals think of their phones as personal objects. In this case, Generations C, Y, and X are more likely to choose their ringtones, wallpaper, and other features, including a range of cell phone holders to match outfits or accommodate purses, belts, or other articles of clothing. In many cases, the cell phone has become a clothing accessory.

Internet Use and the American Public

A good number of adults, particularly in the Boomer years, were initially introduced to the Internet at work. This generation also tends to be the one that traditionally works most and often works the longest number of hours. Since this group was in the vanguard of those introduced to computers at the workplace, it would be interesting to understand whether their jobs changed to become compatible with computers and the Internet, or if the Internet changed the amount of time necessary to complete jobs. Certainly e-mail at work and the growth of home computers and fast Internet connections from the home have contributed to the 24/7 lifestyle for many Boomers, as well as others in the workforce, and the continued blurring of public and private uses of the technology.

Studies of Internet use are very specific to the times at which they were conducted. Many people assume that women don't use the Internet as often as men, but several studies in recent years show that the gender gap is closing, even though men and women, boys and girls, often engage in different activities on the Internet (see Table 3.3).[12]

Several of the categories reported in Table 3.3 will be discussed in subsequent chapters, but what is immediately apparent in this data set is that the most frequent uses of the Internet for all age groups has to do with sending e-mail and getting news. While there are obvious implications for the future of the post office, using

Table 3.3
Online Activities by Age Group

Generational Differences in Online Activities

	Online Teens[a] (12–17)	Gen Y (18–28)	Gen X (29–40)	Trailing Boomers (41–50)	Leading Boomers (51–59)	Matures (60–69)	After Work (70+)	All Online Adults[b]
Go Online	87%	84%	87%	79%	75%	54%	21%	72%
Online games	81	54	37	29	25	25	32	36
School research	*	73	60	61	48	33	14	57
Instant message	75	66	52	38	42	33	25	47
Text message	*	60	44	29	15	11	8	35
Download music	51	45	28	16	14	8	5	25
Read blogs	38	41	30	20	21	19	16	27
Download video	31	27	22	14	8	8	1	18
Create a blog	19	20	9	3	9	3	4	9
Get health info on at least one topic	*	73	84	80	84	68	72	79
Bank online	*	38	50	44	37	35	22	41
Use email	89	88	92	90	94	90	89	91
Get news	76	72	76	75	70	74	68	73
Online purchase	43	68	69	68	67	65	41	67
Participate in an online auction	*	26	29	25	20	18	6	24

[a] Source for Online Teens data: Pew Internet & American Life Project Teens and Parents Survey, Oct.–Nov. 2004. Margin of error is ±4% for online teens.
[b] Source for Online Adult data: Pew Internet & American Life Project surveys conducted in January 2005, May–June 2005, and September 2005. Margin of error for all online adults is ±3% for these surveys. Questions pertaining to health topics, government sites, and religious info were asked in November 2004. Margin of error for that survey is ± 5% for all online adults. The average margin of error for each age group, which can be considerably higher than ±5%, is listed in the methodology.

Source: Susannah Fox and Mary Madden, "Generations online," Pew Internet & American Life Project, December 1, 2005, http://www.pewinternet. org/pdfs/PIP_generations_memo.pdf, 3. Accessed March 11, 2006. Used with permission.

wired and cell phones for communication, and how news is presented, along with the future of the newspaper, radio, and television news industries, the most apparent feature of these categories is speed of information. The growth of blogs as a source of information (whether they reflect fact or opinion, and whether the user can differentiate the two) has great potential to change what people know as well as how they know it.

Perhaps what is most surprising in the study is the representation of older generations in the categories of using games, banking online, and making purchases online. While we might expect older users to search for health care information on the Internet, it is somewhat surprising to see younger users also seeking this type of information. We can probably assume, though, that the type of health care information each generation seeks is a bit different.

Table 3.3 also shows that Internet users are searching for a wider range of services. As the study's narrative suggests, one reason that more people may be using the Internet for more personal uses is that more now have access to broadband technology to deliver high-speed Internet access to the home.[13] These data have been corroborated by a *Harris Interactive Poll* finding that more than half (54%) of the Internet users in America have broadband connections that deliver high-speed Internet services to the home. Furthermore, the Harris Poll indicates that Internet users are representative of the demographic profile of the nation as a whole, and that women now surpass men in terms of using online services (51% of women compared with 49% of men, without differentiating age groups).[14]

Internet Time and Space

Concepts dealing with time and space are partially influenced by a person's age. Certainly there is no doubt that ten minutes to a four-year-old who is being punished with a "time out" can be an interminably long time, while ten minutes of solitude to a busy mother can be nirvana. But technological time is different. If you use a dial-up connection to access the Internet and then switch to DSL or broadband, you might feel giddy about how fast your messages are transmitted, how much more information you can download, and how quickly the screen fills with information. Concurrently, if you have to pay for these services yourself, you may have to make some choices about how much you're willing to pay for the luxury of a fast connection.

Instant Messaging (IMing) is another feature that is used by Generations C, Y, and X to a greater extent than other age groups. This feature is inherently interesting for a number of reasons. It exploits the real-time transfer of data, but can also be asynchronous, since it takes some time to write a response to a message that has just shown up on your screen. There is an assumption of interactivity as an illusion of synchronicity, but there is, actually, a necessary delay in the act of typing a response. This has led to yet another shortcut for communication purposes and a language that makes instant messaging more comfortable for the user (see Table 3.2). At the same time, however, it institutes a level of informality in instant messaging that may not be appropriate for communication between different generations. While abbreviations and shortcuts may be appropriate for social interaction, the style and technique doesn't translate well to e-mails that might be received by professors, bosses, or other authority figures. When a student writes to a professor with a message such as "hey jarice-?ru? I ned 2CU," the informality of the language can appear to a professor to be disrespectful as well as offensive. When it comes to professor/student communication, these abbreviations also lead the professor to wonder whether the student is literate or is just using the features of the technology.

Internet Public and Private Use

Since there are so many generational approaches to thinking about the role of computers and the Internet today, it is understandable that members of Generations C and Y haven't learned appropriate protocols for contacting authority figures in other generations. The informality that they have grown up with and that their technology exploits seems natural to them. Learning that there are appropriate forms of communication and address for different people is part of growing up, but there hasn't been a place in traditional school curricula, or home coaching to take this type of socialization into consideration. As I counsel students to think of how they represent themselves on the Internet, I remind them that potential employers are probably not going to be impressed by an e-mail address that belongs to "booger21."

The blurring of formal and informal styles and activities that have traditionally been the domain of either public or private places becomes more apparent as the Internet becomes used for more social activities. Social networking through services like *Facebook*, *Friendster*, or *MySpace* raises the question of whether relationships can be established and maintained online, and whether these types of social interactions are as fulfilling as face-to-face interactions. This subject is covered in greater depth in later chapters, but the idea that some human needs can be fulfilled on the Internet is a provocative one that impacts the amount of time someone might spend on the Internet for fun or for leisure. This raises the important question of whether people's social skills change when communicating over various forms of media, and whether this then affects values, behaviors, and attitudes. Some critics of contemporary culture claim that the alienating effects of living in the postmodern age drive individuals to withdraw from face-to-face social interaction, and avoid the possibility of interpersonal conflict in social settings. Some people experience a level of social anxiety in face-to-face situations, and actively choose what they perceive of as a safer type of interaction that allows them to control the amount of "closeness" they can feel toward someone over an Internet connection.

THE DIGITAL DIVIDE: THE HAVE-NOTS AND DON'T WANTS

As indicated at the beginning of this chapter, the digital divide is a term traditionally associated with people who have not had access to digital communication technologies because of their own socioeconomic status or the lack of available infrastructure to support using cell phones or the Internet. Most discussions of the digital divide result in discussions of class, race, and political power, or lack of political power.

It might be surprising to find that there is very little difference among cell phone users of different races across the United States[15] and that while there have been extreme gaps in access to computer technologies and the Internet for people of nonwhite races and ethnicities, many of these gaps have been closing. For years, African Americans have trailed Hispanics and whites (who had similar patterns of access) in Internet use, but the fastest adopters in recent years are African Americans.[16] Persons with disabilities and those who don't speak English tend to have less access to the Internet, and the number of people who say they have never used the Internet comprises about 22 percent of the population.[17]

Along with those who don't have access to either cell phones or the Internet, there are those who, like Robert J. Samuelson (quoted earlier in this chapter), choose not to have cell phones or use the Internet. In a Pew Internet and American Life Project study on "Digital Divisions," Susannah Fox questioned why some people preferred not to use the Internet. She found:

32% of non-users say they are just not interested in going online
31% of non-users say they simply do not have access
7% of non-users say they are too busy or think going online is a waste of time
6% of non-users say getting access is too difficult or frustrating
5% of non-users say getting access is too expensive[18]

What happens to those people who either don't have access to cell phones, or the Internet, or even to those who don't care about using them? Do they really miss out on significant experiences? Certainly one set of issues arises when the digital divide discriminates against people and prevents them from making a living or getting an education or participating in the benefits of online information, but when the Internet is used for leisure purposes, the issue of access becomes less important.

One answer is that all of these people can still communicate in other ways. Talking, and getting news by newspapers, radio, and television still exists. Wired telephones still do the job of connecting people to others, and often, without dropped calls or interference. Although the "have-nots" and "don't wants" may be limited in access, they might still be able to communicate through more traditional forms, including conversations. Certainly access to technology is important, but the lifestyles of individuals and their preferences for how they communicate are equally as compelling for the analysis of who may suffer and who may be just fine in the digital divide.

DIGITAL THINKING

The data represented in the two studies in this chapter show that though the use of cell phones and the Internet is growing for members of all generations, those groups differentially use the features delivered by the technologies. Generations C, Y, and X understand digital logic and can exploit the features of digital communication. Members of these generations often generate many of the new uses for these media. So if these younger members of society are leading the way, what characteristics might we expect to see emerging in our culture in the future?

Digital technology leads people to think and act more spontaneously. The immediate nature of both cell phones and the Internet and the ability to reach people quickly, through spontaneous calls, text messaging, or instant messaging, leads people to feel that they are communicating more frequently, but the nature of the communication experience may be different than face-to-face communication. Texting and IMing are void of emotion, and even adopting abbreviated languages such as emoticons (those used for Internet communication) and shorthand (for text messaging over cell phones) contributes to the lack of depth of communication and reduces the message to an even more symbolic nature.

The attitudes of different generations toward the utility of cell phones and the Internet become very personal expressions of how people use these technologies on a daily basis. Rather than reacting to the forms of mass media that are still present in our culture today, cell phones and the Internet have become more portable, and more personal technologies and services. As they become more pervasive, we can expect to see fewer audiences spending time with traditional mass media, and more time with personal technologies that can distribute older types of media content, and new types that exploit the features of more personal technologies. It's not that the "mass" audience no longer exists—it's just that the economic forces of the traditional industries are changing, and cell phones and the Internet are two drivers of that change.

The remaining chapters of this book examine this time in history to see how, where, when, and why cell phones and the Internet have introduced new situations that exploit both the features of the technology and the people who use them. What emerges is a cultural landscape shaped by new concepts of time and space, and public and private behaviors that will define generations to come.

Time Bandits and Space Cadets: Intimacy and Illusions of Control

Cell phones and the Internet are technologies that impose a sense of time over the user that is very different than that of "mass" media. We use these technologies for a number of interactions that involve us at such a personal level that it's easy to lose track of time. The convenience of a cell phone makes it possible to chat or leave a message on the spur of a moment, and we can blast off an e-mail or instant message that might just be a fragment of what we're really hoping to communicate, or start surfing the Internet only to realize that we've been wandering around cyberspace longer than we thought we would. Individuals sometimes personalize and immerse themselves in the digital features of the cell phone and the Internet to such a degree that they lose control over the technology or the messages they hope to communicate. As discussed in previous chapters, most people report that they use cell phones to fill free time. When it comes to the Internet, people are often frustrated when they can't quickly find what they're looking for or are surprised when they find that they've been lulled into browsing the Internet longer than they thought they might. The very characteristics that lead people to believe that cell phones and the Internet help them control their time and activities can ultimately result in the reality that many just have the *illusion* of control. When that happens it feels as though the technology is robbing us of time, and addictive or other dysfunctional behaviors may be the result. When we lose ourselves in the technologically constructed "space" of the Internet, we may feel that we're free from the physical connections to real life and allow ourselves to create a virtual existence that may have no relation to our real lives. The most common example of illustrating the use of the Internet for time control that easily results in loss of control is how people think of and engage in e-mail. In more extreme cases, control issues can result in Internet addictions like online gambling and gaming. When people succumb to the illusion of control, they engage in behaviors that they themselves may have a hard time understanding. This in turn leads to social practices that begin to change expectations and values. This chapter focuses on the way individuals personalize their experiences with cell phones and the Internet and on the illusions of control that influence personal behavior.

Three types of time controls are in play when we use any communication technology: the control by the industries or service providers, the control exerted by the device (the cell phone or the computer connected to the Internet), and the personal investment of time to which users commit when they use the technology. As demonstrated in Chapter 3, different generations approach their own use of these technologies with different purposes or social uses in mind and different expectations for how long the task should take.

We've been conditioned by earlier media to accept some of the industry controls over how mass media operates. Traditional radio and television industries include program formats and schedules for the effective delivery of programs to audiences, and techniques such as instant replays, special effects, or reruns manipulate time and the sequences of space, but all in ways that audiences have come to expect. A good example of one television program that manipulates both is the show *24*. It uses a format based on the premise that the series takes place in a twenty-four-hour day, and each week the hour-long program presents another sequential hour of the twenty-four-hour "day." A digital clock on screen marks the passage of time, and split screens give the impression of simultaneous action in different locations. Viewers are familiar with these techniques and understand how they function and enhance the enjoyment of the story line and the suspense of the show. Although we expect television watching to be structured into logical time frames, *we* also begin to internalize the time sequences of media. This type of conditioning affects all aspects of how we think of time; the result is that we unconsciously begin to behave according to the internalized expectations that we develop when using these technologies.

Most teachers know that certain age groups develop different attention spans according to the type of media they use. Most students today need either a break or some stimulation every twenty minutes or so, which corresponds to the time they'd expect a commercial break on television. Teachers have had to adapt lesson plans to accommodate shifts in attention spans, and even adults generally become uncomfortable when they sit in one place for very long. We're all so familiar with films we see in a movie theater that typically run from ninety minutes to two hours that when we come across a longer film, our bodies react. We might squirm or start to feel that we've been sitting too long, or feel that we need to stretch. But what about personal technologies like cell phones and the way people use computers to access the Internet? They are both available for use 24/7, and the user can choose when and how long to use them, so doesn't the *user* control these technologies? How are these issues of control negotiated? The first step toward the illusion of control is how individuals choose to personalize and think of their technologies.

PERSONALIZING TECHNOLOGIES

Marshall McLuhan often remarked that every technology influences a person's sense ratios. What he meant was that any form of media "extends" our senses according to the way the medium influences the message.[1] If McLuhan were alive today, he'd probably smile at the way people seem to personalize small, portable technologies to reflect their personalities. From choosing a cell phone to suit physical needs or a computer that can be used only by a person who opens it with a digital thumb scan[2] to choosing images, sounds, and accessories, as well as e-mail addresses, these technologies surpass all others in the ways in which people personalize the hardware and think about the personal nature of their use. This in turn becomes a social commentary about how important these technologies are in our culture.

Cell phone manufacturers specifically target certain audiences with features, names, and styles of phones that appeal to different age groups. Certainly a wide range of choices of cell phones is available for different users who might appreciate larger keypad numbers (like the Matures, or Boomers), colors (particularly for the young female users of Generations C, Y, and X), and sporty models that suggest speed and a sleek profile for the athletic or body-conscious user of any age. Cell phone manufacturers have even developed colorful cell phones for the preteen market, and aggressively court teen-aged users.[3] One manufacturer even sells a cell phone that identifies with a flavor (the Chocolate cell phone), and Apple has a range of products that make the consumers feel as though they control the technology. From the iPod and iTunes to the iPhone, Apple has been in the lead for creating and marketing personal technologies.

In addition to personalizing cell phones by choosing ringtones, many cell phone users even assign specific rings so that certain numbers can be identified by sound. Caller identification (ID) functions can even tell who the caller is by name. This often contributes to a change in the nature of the conversation, as the person answering the phone responds with a direct greeting by name rather than saying "Hello" as the standard greeting. When the caller is known, a shorter, more abrupt type of conversation sometimes follows, leading many people to deduce that cell phones contribute to rude behavior. Many people remark that even when inadvertently eavesdropping on someone else's conversation, they feel that many cell phone users bark orders and make demands, further "distancing" themselves from the person at the other end instead of using the phone to socially or emotionally "connect" to someone. The busy executive who calls a staff member from an airport or while in transit can easily get caught up in the pace of travel or the pressure of time and become offensive to subordinates or coworkers (just listen to these conversations sometime!). Shorter, more fragmented conversations reinforce the idea that digital communication is asynchronous or less contextually rich than previous uses of the telephone or what we might expect in face-to-face communication.

Some products can turn the cell phone into a clothing accessory, such as a range of covers that can be changed to match one's outfit or be worn on a belt, or even around the neck. Women's purses now often have an outer pocket for the cell phone, and briefcases and tote bags are often designed with special compartments so that cell phones can be accessed easily. With a cell phone, a person no longer really needs a wristwatch, an address book, or even a photo album. This in turn also leads to the way people think of privacy and the ownership of personal communication as well as personal information. Since phone numbers are not accessible through directory assistance or listed in a book, the cell phone can control one's access to others. One college student who lost his cell phone on a Friday complained on Monday, "I don't know anybody's phone numbers. I had no way to contact my buddies. I had to go out and make new friends."

Even more interesting than the way people wear phones is the way they talk about them. Many people say they "love" their cell phones. Indeed, for a technology that promises so much control over where someone goes, cell phones can simultaneously promise freedom from, and connection to others. As some folks confess to loving their cell phones, many also go farther by personalizing their computers with names and thinking of them as intimate technologies, too. Computers, like cell phones, can also be personalized with screen savers, wallpaper, or sounds that particularly appeal to individual users. Because the computer connects to the Internet for e-mailing, shopping, getting information about health care, and even accessing adult content, people feel that the Internet is practically synonymous with personal communication. People often name their computers the same way they'd name a pet, a car, or a boat. When we anthropomorphize non-human beings, or objects, we make them seem more familiar to us or more like friends. Giving names to inanimate or nonhuman objects is a way of making them seem more like us, and if not more human, at least more "friendly."

TECHNOLOGY AND TIME CONTROL

The technological characteristics of computers, particularly their memory functions, have even more subtle and powerful effects for the user than any other technology. Carl Sagan once wrote that the most intriguing aspect of using computers is that they process information *exsosomatically*—that is, outside of the body.[4] When this happens, the human need for exercising the mental memory is reduced and the computer takes on the function of long-term memory. Many people report that they find something they had written on their computer at a later date, after having forgotten that they wrote it in the first place. The automatic spelling and grammar features of the computer are useful in the process of constructing a document, but they can be dysfunctional when a person never reads the document for clarity, organization, and syntax. When connected to the Internet, the speed of the technology and the "memory" functions sometimes work faster than the human mind can accommodate, and, as with the student who had all of his friends' phone numbers stored on his cell phone, the reliance on the features of the technology (or at least its memory functions) can sometimes reduce the need for an alternative backup of information, only to leave you with data you can't find again or can easily forget.

How fast we can make a connection or find what we want influences our attitudes about whether using the technologies are useful and pleasurable, or not. Sometimes time structures are imposed by industrial controls, such as when cell phone packages come in allotments of minutes, with an incentive for people to speak at certain times of the day or night when their charges are "free." Some packages allow users to roll over unused minutes from one month to another, creating a bank of time that is similar to a savings account and reinforcing the idea that one has "saved time."

Other features are often embedded in the technology. The time it takes for a cell phone to connect to a network after turning it on, or the amount it takes for a computer to connect to the Internet service provider, can seem interminable when someone is in a hurry. The users' willingness to wait for a connection is usually related to how important they feel it is to make a call or access information. People with dial-up modems are sometimes shocked at how much faster they can access the Internet once they get broadband technologies into the home, and few ever go back to dial-up systems, unless they use the Internet rarely or don't care about receiving large files with pictures, graphics, or sound. Of course, where and why one uses the computer to access the Internet significantly influences one's concept of time. The home consumer may use the Internet for casual browsing, but when the Internet is being used for work, a quick response may be a necessity, especially when a worker's productivity is measured against the clock. Members of Generations C, X, and Y often complain that even a lag of two seconds is too long to wait while accessing information on the Internet,[5] which gives credibility to the idea that the pace of society may be speeding up.

Even when it may take a bit longer than people would like to connect to services over their cell phones or the Internet, they become conditioned to instant communication and quick reactions. As the technologies introduce new ways of communicating, we sometimes don't realize how our routine use of technologies begins to influence our behaviors. When people internalize these time structures, they adopt behaviors and beliefs to model their technologies. The use of cell phones has been blamed for people developing bad habits about getting to meetings or social obligations on time, because many people feel that their rude or bad behavior will be excused if they call to explain why they're running late.[6] Nowhere is this more apparent than in the use of e-mail, which is the single biggest reason why people use the Internet for both business and for pleasure.

E-MAIL TROUBLES

The wonderful features of e-mail are easy to observe: low-cost messages that go anywhere within only fractions of seconds and leave an electronic "trail" of interactions are examples of some of the positive functions, but sometimes the amount of e-mail one receives and the length of time it takes to respond to all of the messages makes it seem that e-mail could possibly be overused, at least some of the time. Many people treat the opening of the e-mail as the first ritual of the day, either at home or at work. For many, the following few hours can be easily spent responding to important and not-so-important questions, and most people tend to answer them in sequence. Usually they feel compelled to finish everything in the "in-box" in one sitting so as to feel good about keeping up with the volume of messages. Since most people organize their e-mail in a certain order, they may find that they spend an inordinate amount of time answering a message, only to find that someone has sent them a later message telling them "never mind." When the messages aren't organized in a way that allows scanning them first according to sequence, they can get lost or be forgotten. This is very likely to happen when the computer is thought of as a "memory" technology and the users forget that *they* have to remember to check their files. What is also lost is hours of trying to stay current, when some of the interactions are so minor that you sometimes feel that you've wasted hours just trying to wade through the minutia of the day. This sense of immediacy and the fragmentation that emerges from answering message after message contributes to the temporary nature of e-mail. Responses may be quick, but perhaps not thorough, or even thoughtful. If an incoming message asks for reactions to three items, someone who is trying to get through the list of mail quickly may only respond to one answer and press the "send" button. Since there is no record of the interaction unless you seek it out, the message (or nonresponse to items in a message) can easily be forgotten. Seldom do many people return to previous message to make sure they've answered everything fully, because the system leads them to think that once they've pushed the "reply" button, they've done their part. The sense of accomplishment they have in completing the in-box of e-mail quickly goes away when, in twenty minutes, the in-box is loaded with another set of mail.

The idea of keeping up with the sequential list of e-mail is a time-related problem. When e-mail messages aren't answered promptly, it can appear that some people are not doing their job. People who do not answer messages promptly can appear to be disinterested in the person who sent the message. To make sure that the in-box is emptied regularly, many workers take their work home and spend hours on e-mail in their own time. Whether this is a problem or not depends on the pressure of the job and the philosophy of the employers. E-mail, more than any other Internet feature, contributes to the 24/7 nature of never leaving the workplace. Furthermore, the ease of sending e-mail sometimes comes at the expense of conversing with a colleague at work. Some employers have even limited employees from using e-mail among coworkers in order to encourage face-to-face interpersonal communication and foster a friendlier workplace.[7]

One could speculate that most chain letters, jokes, and urban legends that circulate through the Internet for years are probably the result of people in the workplace who have a bit of time to fill, but for most workers who experience time pressure when they check messages, these items often result in a quick "delete" stroke. Handling spam, the unwanted, often annoying e-mail messages that clog electronic mailboxes, and cleaning up viruses and other unwanted messages is a very annoying feature of using the Internet and makes people feel that the technology drains their time and highlights their loss of control over the technology.

The social impact of e-mail is also something tied to different generations. Young people (Generations C and Y in particular) often send text messages, rather than e-mail, at least to their own peers. These users think of e-mail as reserved for contacting professors, employers, or older people who don't use text messaging. Regardless of age, though, many people are often shocked to find that the contents of e-mail are not their exclusive property. When this happens, embarrassing, or costly mistakes can result in several surprises for the dedicated e-mail user. Where someone uses e-mail and over what system dictates how severe the problem may be.

SPACE AND PLACE

Thinking that e-mail is personal property is most often a problem when home and work use becomes blurred. Many anecdotes are told about employees who get fired when the boss confronts them with using e-mail, shopping, gambling, accessing pornography, or just for using the computer at work for too many personal reasons. This idea of personal space and use extends to what gets stored on a computer owned by someone else too. People often feel that what they store on a hard drive is personal property, rather than company property, and often forget that the system used to access the Internet in any place other than the home is "controlled" by policies related to use. College students seem shocked when they receive a notice from a school suspending their Internet privileges because there's evidence that the student downloaded too much music or too much porn. Rather than being surprised that there might be penalties for accessing this type of information, they are more surprised that their activities were monitored by the school, when they thought what they were doing was personal, private, and secure, all reasonable expectations when using the same technology in the home.

Obviously, cell phones also reflect social structures when they liberate someone from using a wired phone. The idea that a call can be made from anywhere and the person called may not know where the caller is calling from is one such feature. Many jokes have been made about a phone call to a boss, a spouse, or a teacher, allegedly purporting that the caller is in one location, only to find later that the person could not have been where he or she claimed to have been. Even the survey in Chapter 3 shows that many people (young and old) occasionally lie about where they are when using cell phones. Similarly, because of the portable nature of cell phones and calling services, the idea of long-distance calls and area codes no longer really seems to matter. College students who live away from home and use only cell phones might ask a teacher to call and leave a number that requires a long-distance charge, because the phone package is held in the student's home state.

When it comes to the space-shifting nature of the Internet, volumes have been written about conceptualizing *cyberspace* and the concept of "place" that no longer exists geographically, but metaphorically. Even if the space can't be described in physical terms, the effect on how we might unconsciously or uncritically think of space still matters. James Beniger describes cyberspace as "consist[ing] not only of material things like people and their artifacts (computers, modems, telephone lines, etc.)" but also of the "relationships among individuals, and the cybercultural contents of their heads—the sense of belonging to cyberspace, and what that might mean."[8] Many studies of cyberspace seek to explore what happens to the individual's sense of identity in cyberspace, including the idea that cyberspace can "free" people from the confines of their own physical bodies or their real-world physical space. No matter where the user is, what goes on in cyberspace is a personal matter that is characterized by informality of communication, fragmentation of meaning, and a sense of disconnection from the physical body or the physical real world. Even if it has never happened to you, everyone has known about someone who starts playing a game on the Internet and seems to forget about real time, real people, and real situations. Even if the experience is only a short one, the power of the Internet and programs that transport us to cyberspace have unique characteristics when it comes to time and space. Cell phone and Internet addictions and the use of gaming demonstrate the consequences of a person's loss of time and place.

ADDICTIVE BEHAVIOR AND THE ILLUSION OF CONTROL

Because cell phones and the Internet are personal communication forms and can be further personalized, loved, and relied upon, it's not far-fetched for some people to develop unhealthy or dysfunctional habits. In recent years the concept of Internet addiction has become a bona fide clinical phenomenon, as evidenced by scholarly approaches to understanding who are the most vulnerable, how they become addicts, and the need for serious treatment for this type of abuse. In the case of Internet addiction, the American Psychological Association has defined the problem as a situation in which individuals manifest a loss of control over the time they spend on the Internet despite deteriorating effects upon their lives, such as in personal relationships.[9] As an addictive technology, they may substitute real personal interactions with others and offer the illusion of control for their users. At this time in history, more attention has been given to the addictive potential presented by the Internet than cell phones, largely because of the discussion surrounding the content matter of Internet addiction. But as cell phones become more sophisticated—and as we move from second-generation to third-generation phones, the range of activities available on cell phones will soon grow to rival that of Internet. Because cell phones are increasingly becoming capable of connecting to the Internet, it's a matter of time before all of the same programs and services that can lead one to Internet addiction become available to cell phone users, too. *The New York Times* columnist Joel Conarroe wrote about the ubiquitous technology that he claims shows an addiction to talking:

> While sitting in a coffee shop the other day, I had an epiphany. Surrounded by men and women cuddling their cell phones, it struck me that these

little metallic instruments are this millennium's cigarette. Just a few years ago my fellow coffee drinkers would have been smoking. . . . Now they're clutching phones. Between courses, and the end of a meal, folks used to light up. . . . Before the cell phone, theatergoers rushed to the lobby during intermissions simply for a quick smoke. Now they hurry out to shout (the "cell yell," it's called) into their indispensable gadgets.[10]

While the perceived need to talk may well be a part of an addictive pathology, both the nature of the talk and what the constant connection means are far more telling of how cell phones may be used. The portability and convenience of cell phones allows one to express a thought at a moment's notice, rather than waiting for the opportunity for another type of interaction, but Americans often respond that they know they are using their cell phones to fill any free time they may have.[11] Even when the push to fill time supersedes the desire to control time, the feeling that instant communication can be attainable anywhere, anytime, helps explain why many people feel they must be available and accessible 24/7, and why they feel other people should be too. We know that all media is habitual, so when people do rely on the cell phone for talking or any other activity, the potential for addiction is present.

One of the first and most notable psychologists to diagnose the problem of Internet addiction is Kimberly S. Young, who writes about her three-year study of Internet addicts in the book *Caught in the Net: How to Recognize the Signs of Internet Addiction—and a Winning Strategy*. Often, the behavior is first noticed by family members or friends, who realize that someone they care about is connected to the Internet more often than usual, which results in the neglect of work, school, or other relationships. According to Young, Internet addiction is like any other compulsive behavior, such as gambling, chronic overeating, sexual compulsions, or obsessive television watching. She writes that often people become addicted to particular features of the Internet, such as chat rooms, interactive games, or shopping programs such as e-Bay. A good number of problems seem to be related to sexual content, because the Internet also offers a level of anonymity for users. Her claim that sexual content is one of the more addictive features of the Internet is corroborated by other researchers,[12] and this too underscores the notion that the computer and Internet are used for some of the most personal reasons. A compelling study about Korean Internet users suggests that Internet addicts also seem to be more vulnerable to interpersonal relationships than others and that they have an unusually close feeling to strangers,[13] a factor that may frighten any parents who wonder what their children are doing on the Internet!

Young describes the type of people who most often lose personal control over their Internet use:

> I've found that some form of escape usually lies at the heart and soul of the drive toward Internet addiction. Many of these people are depressed and lonely, held back by low self-esteem, insecurity, and anxiety. Maybe they're unhappy in their relationships, or their jobs, or their social life. A few are battling diseases like cancer, or living with a permanent disability. Teenagers who succumb to the Internet's pull often say they're misunderstood by their parents and feel trapped at home.[14]

While Young and others write about how certain Internet services can seduce users of all ages, college-age students might be particularly susceptible, because when they go away to college, they not only have free access to the Internet, but they have blocks of unstructured time, may feel some social anxiety in a new place, and are often away from parents or anyone else who might monitor their Internet use for the first time. Added to all of these social pressures is the reality that faculty members often encourage the students to use the Internet for other purposes as well, such as research, fact checking, and submitting assignments.[15] Young cites Provost W. Richard Ott, who claimed that in one year at Alfred University in New York, 43 percent of the freshmen had been dismissed because of Internet abuse,[16] and he claimed that the Internet was being used for "self-destruction."

Most addictive and compulsive behaviors on the Internet result in uncontrolled personal time, as the user searches for an escape from reality. Addictions to sex chat rooms or pornography could signal a desire to escape from an unsatisfying relationship, a lack of self-esteem, or loneliness. The ability to be anonymous or to choose a different identity in these interactions further distances people from their real selves and may seem to free them from the characteristics in their real identities. In extreme cases, the result can be the creation of a fantasy life that becomes even more important and more satisfying to the person than real life. When this happens, the theorists who claim that video games actually function as a substitution for real interactions seem to have grasped one concept about the digital world that others merely gloss over.

GAMBLING, GAMING, AND GRATIFICATION

The many types of video games make it difficult to predict exactly who would be most likely to feel the extraordinary impact of spending time in virtual space, but all evidence points to the reality that people who spend a significant amount of time online are the most likely to *think* of their interactions as significant components of their lives. Like watching television, playing video games becomes habitual; the sense of time and space that results is influenced by the technology and the person's dexterity and skill in understanding the digital logic that codes all games. The investment of time and the comfort with the technology leads people to think that they have personal control over what they do. Whether they do maintain a balance between virtual and real worlds is a matter of their psychological and sociological balance, but for those who feel disassociated from others, the feeling of "aloneness" can result in further alienation and retreat from the real world.

One of the fastest growing industries on the Internet is online gambling. From sports betting to the current fad of gambling on celebrity behavior (will Brad and Angelina's baby be a boy or a girl?), the growth in online gambling has been nothing short of astounding. Most of the online "casinos" are based in other countries besides the United States (it is technically illegal to run an online gambling program in the United States), with many European companies leading the way and countries such as Japan, China, and Malaysia poised to become Internet gambling powerhouses.[17] Furthermore, Internet addicts are much more likely to become Internet gamblers, click on advertisements, and sign up for additional e-mail marketing and e-mail promotions.[18]

The growth in online gambling worldwide has resulted in a 14.5 billion dollar global market, with one-fourth of that amount coming from the United States. Online gambling has become one of the Internet's largest moneymakers, and while most people can enjoy a little harmless wager now and then, the potential for big money and the ease of gambling from home has resulted in a growing number of people who are committed, through habit or addiction, to online gambling. Although the U.S. government has made several attempts to curb or control online gambling, its efforts seem ineffective and doomed. Capitalism has already staked its claim in the high-stakes world of online gambling. American investment houses have begun to provide financial backing for offshore casinos through mutual funds that have brought poker, blackjack, and roulette to the growing number of Internet gamblers,[19] leading to greater availability of these sites and more temptation for those already unable to control their time, impulses, or money. Evidence from a number of studies confirms that the compulsive or addicted Internet gambler also tends to have a psychological propensity toward depression, and possibly substance abuse.[20] The fact that so many people do wager from the privacy of their homes makes it difficult to know who the gamblers are, or even for friends or family to notice the behavior.

One of the key features of the technology that has fueled Internet gambling is the growth of peer-to-peer file sharing, which allows individuals to play over the Internet in real time. While this has attracted users of all ages, the growth in gambling is a part of the extraordinary growth in gaming online, which is now available on many cell phones, too. In the realm of gaming in general, we can see the extraordinary technological control that gamers pit themselves against in their quest to enter cyberspace and exert their own *illusions* of control.

SPACE CADETS

While entire books have been written about the impact of video gaming, it's hard to grasp the overall enormity of the industry and the impact of these games on individuals, because the images conjure different triggers for people of different ages. The term *video game* might suggest an arcade game, a game console that can be connected to a television set, a self-contained unit like a Game Boy, or a software program one can play on a computer. There are even inexpensive games that can be purchased for cell phones that are viewed on the small cell phone screen. Will Wright, *Wired* magazine's guest editor for a special feature on "The New World of Games," summed up the generational attitudes toward gaming when he wrote,

> Society . . . notices only the negative. Most people on the far side of the generational divide—elders—look at games and see a list of ills (they're violent, addictive, childish, worthless). Some of these labels may be deserved. But the positive aspects of gaming—creativity, community, self-esteem, problem-solving—are somehow less visible to nongamers. I think part of this stems from the fact that watching someone play a game is a different experience than actually holding the controller and playing it yourself. Vastly different.[21]

The elements of contemporary online games that are so distinctive have to do with the issues of time, space, and control by the program and the user. Once again, time can be considered in the same way as any browsing period on the Internet. If a person is using video games to learn a new skill, or to fill available time, the purpose defines the relationship between user and time spent on the game. Games can be dysfunctional, however, when they offer a sense of time and space that is so different from reality that the user loses control of how long he or she plays a game. This happens frequently when people immerse themselves in a game. Frequent Internet users, who browse, spend a lot of time in chat rooms, or spend more time on the Internet than in social settings with other people, often become addicted to gaming, too.

Video gaming is another example of a technologically controlled innovation that has evolved over the years, establishing signposts along the path of cultural change. From the simple entertainment arcade games such as Pong to the Atari and Nintendo consoles to today's interactive Internet-based real-time cyberworld games, "videogames are transforming our culture, from sex and sports to medicine and economics."[22] In the context of how video gaming influences users' attitudes and behaviors, the elements of addiction, the illusion of control, and personal investment of people's sense of identity in cyberspace, video games demonstrate how entertainment media can become a much larger component of introducing new attitudes, behaviors, and values to our culture.

As the generational chart in Table 3.3 shows, the age groups most likely to play online games include Generations C, Y, and X. The teens that represent Generation C are among the heaviest users in that study, with 81 percent of the respondents reporting that they play games online. Niche markets for different age groups have emerged. It might be surprising to realize that the over seventy group also plays online games more than the Matures or the Boomers. The reasons for this may have to do with their availability of time, and that interaction with games is a social activity for those who might be alone or housebound. There is little evidence so far to indicate what types of games the over-seventy crowd plays, but it is probably a logical assumption that the games are more of the casino variety than something like Doom or Grand Theft Auto.

For those who think of video games as violent, first-shooter games, it may come as a surprise that games can run the gamut from pro-social games to collaborative team-building exercises with story lines and three-dimenensional "metaverses," where you can change shape, gender, and species.[23] Many games have changed from the early versions of Pong or Space Invaders to allow participants to invent virtual worlds, and the term *metaverse* describes how the special space for playing these games actually gives the impression of a different type of universe, where personal choice (including that of self-identification) can exist. For people who play virtual world games, "games are not just entertainment but a vehicle for self-expression."[24] In 2004, John C. Beck and Mitchell Wade wrote that "Americans now spend more money on video games each year than they do on going to the movies, and more time at home playing video games than watching rented videos."[25] Since 2004, the gaming industry has grown even larger, with revenues in 2005 approximating $7 billion, and a new burst in what is now called the "interactive entertainment" area.[26]

Gaming culture represents a very different generation gap among users. As Beck and Wade write, "It's not just that boomers and gamers grew up differently; those differences have led to very different worldviews."[27] Heavy gamers, particularly those of the C, Y, and X generations, *do* think of time and space differently than their older counterparts. With an innate understanding of digital logic that is different from that of people whose primary forms of entertainment are passive, such as television and film, younger gamers have found ways to integrate features of gaming into other aspects of their lives, thus influencing attitudes and changing their values. For young gamers, fantasy and escape from the real world takes on a different meaning than it might for older users. Whether people choose to call this the cyberspace or the metaverse, the fictional world one enters from the real world has become a distinctly personal space where non-real-world behaviors are encouraged and rewarded. Because the world of the Internet is, by its nature, global, the online games with multiple players can be immersions into different worlds of participation that reflect multiple cultural interpretations and strategies. Several articles have been written that support the idea that rather than escaping from the real world, the heavy online gamer actually uses the games to participate in a widening sense of personal relationships, though there may be no sense of the "body" as a physical entity.

Choosing an identity is also a part of the experience of many online games. Often people can identify themselves in any way they wish, including a choice of race, ethnicity, and identity. Games that involve multiple users and metaverses often encourage the users to design and employ avatars, or animated representations of the self, that might obfuscate the players' real identities. As a result, the users can project themselves into a fantasy world with whatever identity they choose.

There is no doubt that sometimes a foray into a fantasy world can be refreshing and a welcome relief from the real world, but just as in Internet addiction, the line between how people control their time and digital thinking can lead to an illusion of control. While there are many ways in which gamer philosophy and strategies have begun to cross over into other aspects of social life (explored in later chapters), there are some key aspects to understanding what happens when heavy gamers lose control over the amount of time they spend online. The most important feature, as demonstrated by online gaming, is that people can easily feel that they have control over the technology, when they don't. The second feature is that they may feel that their actions (such as when playing video games in a nonreal place like cyberspace or the metaverse) have no consequences. When using games for entertainment, this idea may be fine, but when addictive behavior leads someone to gamble, shop, or indulge so much that the personal life suffers, the game is over.

Five

Digital Democracy: Individuals and Society in Transition

Within hours of the execution of Saddam Hussein on December 30, 2006, graphic images and disturbing sounds recorded by a cell phone were distributed globally over the Internet. The brutality of the act and the words of a bystander, repeated by Saddam to "go to hell," resulted in the last public image of a man who had been hanged for his actions as a dictator. The gruesome images cast Saddam as a martyr to his believers, and even those who despised him registered discontent at seeing his last moments so reduced to such a display. This was not the first time that images and sound had been recorded by bystanders and posted on the Internet. Other examples include pictures of a UCLA student tasered by police, the London Underground bombings, and prisoner abuse at Abu Ghraib Prison, all circulated around the world via the Internet, resulting in shaping public opinion and fueling media content for months and years.[1] In each case, either soldiers or private citizens caught the action and posted the images without editors, publishers, or other gatekeepers making decisions about their propriety, journalistic value, or explanation that might have given context or "balance" to the news. In each of these cases, though, the power of digital cell phones and cameras to unobtrusively record events and distribute them within moments to a global audience demonstrate how digital technologies can challenge traditional journalism to give people news and shape public opinion.

Traditional news media in the United States have been called the "watchdog" of the government, and the media undoubtedly play a role in shaping individuals' knowledge of governmental affairs as well as what it means to be American and live in a democratic society. This chapter addresses the role of cell phones and the Internet as technologies that facilitate instantaneous personal expression and information distributed by individuals for the purposes of influencing public opinion and operating according to democratic principles of freedom of expression. The overall theme is that cell phones and the Internet can be used to create common bonds that tie individuals to a larger community, the country, and in some cases the world. They can challenge authority, such as that of the government or of the media, and they can increase the number of viewpoints available to shape public opinion. The digital communication features of both of these technologies give individuals the opportunity to be creators and disseminators of news and events that reach large audiences. In many cases, they have contributed to changing traditional political practices and offered new ideas for reaching people and facilitating political discourse. The political repercussions of using these new communication forms is part of the ongoing evolution of journalism and democracy in the United States, and they raise some of the most basic assumptions about living in a democracy.

LEGISLATIVE BACKGROUND: MEDIA MADNESS

From the early days of the emerging United States, the relationship of the media and the government has been complimentary at times, and sometimes controversial. Though the history of journalism is full of colorful characters and combative critics, the people of the United States have relied on the media to tell them what to think about, how to interpret political events, and how to make sense of the vicissitudes and polarities of public opinion. Because the media are so powerful, governments often try to control them.

In the formative months and years of the nation, the British government attempted to control dissent and controversy by demanding that printing presses be licensed. Their desire to trace seditious or rabble-rousing content to a specific printer and to punish those who upset the controls of British rule resulted in the actions of the authors of the Constitution to clarify the protections of the new government in the First Amendment to the Constitution, guaranteeing, "Congress shall make no law respecting an establishment of religion, or prohibiting the free exercise thereof; or abridging the freedom of speech, or of the press; or of the right of the people peaceably to assemble, and to petition the Government for a redress of grievances." Freedoms of speech and of the press have guided the behavior of print and broadcast journalists and have been reflected in the efforts of federal agencies such as the Federal Communications Commission (FCC) to craft policies and procedures that respect these freedoms. Our legal institutions, including the Supreme Court, have often invoked these freedoms, but this is not to say that free speech and a free press have always resulted in an uncomplicated relationship between media and society. There have been many legislative battles over *whose* freedoms are at stake when the media have such an important role in making connections between the people and the government. As Robert McChesney, a leading author on media and the democratic process wrote,

> Participatory self-government, or democracy, works best when at least three criteria are met. First, it helps when there are not significant disparities in economic wealth and property ownership across the society. . . . Second, it helps when there is a sense of community and a notion that an individual's well-being is determined to no small extent by the community's well-being. . . . Third, democracy requires that there be an effective system of political communication, broadly construed, that informs and engages the citizenry, drawing people meaningfully into the polity.[2]

Almost every federal review of the media industries prior to deregulation in 1984 considered the rights of the public to information and the desire for diversity of viewpoints as a guideline for legislation. From the first attempt to regulate the use of the electromagnetic spectrum in 1927, the federal position on the use of airwaves for communication purposes was that the spectrum was limited; in order to encourage potential broadcasters to reflect a variety of viewpoints, licenses were required for the operation of any radio transmitter. By the time the Communications Act of 1934 was passed, the newly established FCC began to require that all broadcasters demonstrate that they were operating in the public interest, convenience, and necessity. Ownership of newspapers, radio stations, and, later, television stations was limited, so that one broadcaster or newspaper publisher couldn't exercise too much control over the amount of media in any market. As new technologies began to be developed, including the 1967 development of using the FM range of electromagnetic frequencies, and satellites introduced the possibility of using microwaves for communication purposes, the old arguments favoring the scarcity of the spectrum began to crumble. By the end of the 1970s, cable television, a wired system that did *not* use airwaves, was beginning to present a different model of communication that didn't use the spectrum at all. The new cable television industry remained unregulated by the FCC because it didn't fit the model of broadcasting that had justified the spectrum scarcity argument. As other technologies such as the VCR, videodisc, and videotape were developed, the FCC judged that consumers were able to access different types of content in different forms of non-broadcast media. The rules of regulation were being undermined, and other communications entrepreneurs as well as those who had been limited by ownership restrictions wanted to compete in different forms of media distribution.

The deregulatory atmosphere resulted in the breakup of AT&T, which had held the monopoly on telephony in the United States. The divestiture of the Bell Operating Companies allowed the newly formed regional Baby Bells to begin to compete in the areas of telephone service and value-added services such as caller ID, voice mailboxes, cell phones, and now, content for cell phones. The new "marketplace rules"[3] resulted in greater competition among technology companies and media content providers, and the FCC began a series of modifying ownership requirements that were intended to increase competition, but resulted in a series of corporate takeovers, mergers, and the growth of what became known as "big" media.

By the time the Telecommunications Act of 1996 was passed, a plethora of new communications technologies had emerged, and a new philosophy replaced the idea that the airwaves belong to the people. To be blunt, the "freedom of speech," which had long been a tenet of the philosophy of safeguarding the public airwaves and delivering a multiplicity of viewpoints, became the freedom of speech for those who owned a broadcast license or media business. No longer did the scarcity argument seem relevant, since Americans were actually able to receive what was thought to be a broad range of viewpoints, and it was assumed that a diverse group of owners would assure delivery of a range of content. In actuality, however, the owners' own political influence, which tended toward conservatism, resulted in fewer diverse viewpoints. Since 2004, any media owner (individual or corporate) may own 39 percent of the media outlets in any given market.[4] The effect of this change in philosophy reflects changes in American culture. Today the institutions of media have irrevocably changed and now safeguard the rights of media owners more than the rights of viewers or listeners.

The philosophy behind deregulation was sound, but political forces in play altered the direction of the purpose of deregulation. If, as Mark Fowler and Daniel Brenner opined in their persuasive argument for deregulation, opening up the industries to market forces would deliver a wider range of content options to audiences, and more competition in distribution channels of communication and information would keep costs down, the idea of deregulation might have worked.[5] Instead, major media organizations bought up many of the smaller outlets. We now have a media landscape in which the radio conglomerate Clear Channel owns 90 percent of the radio stations across the country, and many independent newspapers have been unable to survive the dominance of the bigger chains.

To many who are concerned about media conglomeration, the restricted voices and viewpoints available to consumers are most harmful when it comes to news and public affairs. After deregulation and changes in media ownership, many defenders of the role that media play in a democracy warned that the public would suffer from the control of media content by so few organizations that the public would be fed only corporate viewpoints designed to promote corporate ideology and not offend the public. Bill Moyers claimed that "media conglomeration ... takes the oxygen out of democracy."[6] While our mass media were undergoing change, the Internet quietly began to grow and claim the territory that had once been the national meeting place. The Internet seemed to have no limitations in size, and by the time MP3 technology was developed, allowing individuals to post graphics, audio, and video on the Internet, a new forum for public postings, debates, conversations, and controversy had emerged.

In his 2005 keynote address at the "We Media Conference" in New York City, Al Gore, no stranger to the "information superhighway,"[7] commented on how he perceived that American democracy was "in grave danger." He discussed how the founding fathers of our representative democracy relied on "a well-informed citizenry," but that over the years, though our founders were of a world dominated by print media, today's citizen lived in an environment dominated by the one-way nature of television. Gore discussed how the corporate takeover of television, radio, and other forms of mass media had stifled public discussion, and he concluded by extolling the potential of the Internet to return us to an environment in which open dialogue could take place: "We must ensure by all means possible that this medium of democracy's future develops in the mold of the open and free marketplace of ideas that our Founders knew was essential to the health and survival of freedom."[8]

THE ELECTRONIC SOAPBOX: BLOGGING

In many ways blogs are examples of what the Internet can do best by opening up opportunities to post different viewpoints and offering a low-cost alternative for individuals to participate in a broader dialogue about any number of topics. Blogs, or web logs, are postings to the Internet that can range from highly polished professionally produced packages of information that are updated daily, to amateurish, personal musings that appear once, or just at a blogger's whim. There have been some situations in which bloggers actually scooped the traditional media and contributed to the news for the nation, proving that bloggers can sometimes get access to information faster, more easily, and without having to go through a number of gatekeepers, such as editors or publishers. The blogger Matt Drudge was the first to leak information about the President Clinton/Monica Lewinski affair in 1998,[9] starting the firestorm that eventually resulted in Clinton's impeachment. After airing a story on *60 Minutes II*, CBS posted memos on its Web site allegedly proving George W. Bush had received preferential treatment while serving in the Texas Air National Guard. Within minutes, a blogger at the conservative *FreeRepublic.com* site raised a question about the documents' validity, and within hours, other bloggers began to document the mounting evidence of the documents' forgery.[10]

Some individual bloggers treat their sites as a sort of editorial platform and commit hours to making them look professional. Others treat them like online diaries providing a voyeuristic opportunity for other casual readers to ponder. Personal blogs often range from political platforms to reviews of new technologies and analyses of presidential election issues and results, to personal peregrinations, but whatever the posted information, the Internet allows virtually anyone to participate in what has been called "citizen media." While the blogging phenomenon began around 1994, the future of blogging could be the content that revolutionizes the Internet, or it could become just another outlet for advertising and corporate-controlled information. In the process it is likely that some individuals will explore their potential as electronic journalists, while others will be content to use blogs to establish a greater number of online friends and use the features for greater social interaction. According to the blogger Andrew Sullivan, blogs can be as nuanced and well sourced as traditional journalism, but they have the immediacy of talk radio.[11]

By January 2005, Technorati, a popular blog search engine, estimated that 30,000 to 40,000 blogs were being created a day and that 500,000 posts to blogs were made each day.[12] Blogs are protected by the First Amendment, with the exception of those that exercise hate speech (viewpoints that are intended to foment civil unrest) and obscenity, both being types of blogs that would be likely to be removed by their Internet service providers, and are exempt from First Amendment freedom of speech. But another question looms. With all of this possible information, what do people generally see?

Blogging capitalizes on the technological characteristics of the Web, such as immediacy and rapid access to linked information, but it also demonstrates how search engines such as Google or Yahoo! organize information and present it in a sequence of order that registers the popularity of certain sites by the number of "hits" they get. The result is a menu of what other people have consensually "voted" to see on the basis of the way the information is presented on the site. While the number of available sites (63.2 million blogs, as reported by Technorati, December 31, 2006) may indicate that obviously multiple perspectives must be available on the Internet, the sequencing of information also leads casual browsers to view the same information.

At the risk of reducing years of scholarly work on these questions to a few sound bites, a few truisms have emerged. When people are faced with information overload, they tend to seek opinions and positions that justify their own thoughts.[13]

Instead of feeling overwhelmed by information overload, many people choose to be selective about what they choose to read, and choose options that won't challenge their opinions. The legal scholar Cass Sunstein writes,

> With an increase in options, and a greater power to customize, comes an increase in the range of actual choices. Those choices are likely, in many cases, to be that people will try to find material that makes them feel comfortable, or that is created by and for people like themselves ... of course, many people seek out new topics and ideas. And to the extent that people do, the increase in options is hardly bad on balance; it will, among other things, increase variety, the aggregate amount of information, and the entertainment value of actual choices. But there are serious risks as well. If diverse groups are seeing and hearing different points of view, or focusing on different topics, mutual understanding might be difficult, and it might be hard for people to solve problems that society faces together. . . .
>
> With respect to the Internet, the implication is that groups of people especially if they are like-minded will end up thinking the same thing that they thought before—but in more extreme form.[14]

As a source of information, blogging appears to reach all generations, though again, Generations C, Y, and X tend to browse more often and Generations C and Y are much more likely to create their own blogs (see Table 3.3). A Pew Internet & American Life project surveyed 233 bloggers and found that of their respondents, bloggers tended to be people who get most of their news from the Internet, are major consumers of political news, and often use blog features that enhance community and usability. The report also determined that the bloggers surveyed were racially diverse and evenly split between women and men.[15] Businesses also know that there is a growing audience for accessing this information, and virtually every broadcaster, newspaper, or news organization posts a version of its own blog, desiring to cultivate return readers and hoping to entice them to notice the advertising on each blog page.

Can blogs become the new electronic soapbox for different views? In theory, yes. At the same time there are companies that see the commercial potential for blogging to reach audiences with advertising to accompany the blogs, and they, too, have the potential to contribute to direct market advertising and, possibly, overwhelm the user with pop-ups, animated characters, and fast, flashing images to attract the consumer's eye. With messages directed to individuals on their computer screens, the ability to count the number of hits to the blog, and the low cost of delivering ads (between $1 and $12 per thousand impressions),[16] advertising can be lucrative for the blogger as well as for the advertisers. But as a form of citizen media, blogs make the Internet as a lending library of information.

PODCASTING AS PARTICIPATION

When podcasting became available in the year 2000, the optimistic outlook was that once again a technology might be developed that would literally allow any citizen to become a broadcaster. The disc jockey Adam Curry of MTV became the first public figure to use the podcasting service developed by Dave Winer, a software developer.[17] Podcasting does not require a license, because it uses online systems to transfer information and there is no use of the electromagnetic spectrum. Through an aggregator, which functions like an organizer of audio information, the message is packaged for delivery to any technology that uses MP3 compression (the most commonly used is an iPod). The transferring of media files is relatively efficient and inexpensive. The result is a subscription service that regularly downloads audio information, though video podcasts are now possible too because of downloading technologies like the iPod Nano, which has increased capacity capable of compressing video as well as audio signals.

The term "podcasting" has a few possible origins. Because iPods were some of the first technologies available for downloading information, the "pod" designation makes sense. The term was also suggested by Ben Hammersley in the British newspaper the *Guardian* on February 12, 2004. By October of that year a number of detailed articles explaining how to podcast began to appear online, and in November 2004, the first podcast service provider offering storage, bandwidth, and creation tools became available. Since that time, a number of services and systems have become available, of which many are free and downloadable from the Internet. In 2005, the *New Oxford American Dictionary* named "podcast" the word of the year.[18] Since then, a number of other pod-related terms have entered our vocabulary.

Podcasting also brings the baggage of mainstream radio content to the media landscape. Traditional conflict over the ownership of music has plagued more powerful podcasters, but there are now many recordings available to a wider audience designated as a "podsafe." In 2005 the term "podmercial" was used by radio broadcasters in Las Vegas who also distributed the station's signal through a podcast. As might be expected, it didn't take long for podnography to become one of the offerings, and sexcasts quickly followed. A Google search for "adult podcast" showed that on a specific date in 2005, 6,800 adult podcasts (also known as sexcasts) were available.[19]

Traditional broadcasters have readily accepted podcasting as an additional distribution medium. *Fortune*, the *Washington Post*, the *Economist*, the *New York Times*, C-SPAN, and the Fox television network are just a few of the early adopters of podcasting, and the White House sends podcasts in different languages. But despite this alternative delivery system for mainstream media and those with special interests, celebrity podcasts seem to get the most consistent number of downloads. In 2006 the *Guinness Book of Records* noted that the most popular podcast in 2006 was the Ricky Gervais show. In July 2005 the first People's Choice podcast awards were held during the Podcast Expo, where the awards were presented in twenty categories. It is likely that the primary reason for so many mainstream and special-interest broadcasters to also podcast is the hope that while the podcast audiences may be small, they actually provide excellent niche audiences for advertisers, so these podcasts also do not circumvent any commercial sponsorship issues.

It is difficult to accurately assess the number of podcasts available and their listenership/user statistics. Bridge Ratings estimates that by the end of 2005, about 5 million people had heard at least one podcast, though a much smaller number (about 1.6% of the population) actually podcast themselves.[20] The most dramatic growth of the new form accompanied the increase in iPod sales throughout 2005 (about 6 million per quarter in 2005), which fueled a rapid growth in the number of podcasts, from about 1,000 to 26,000 feeds in that year.[21] A quick look at podcastdirectory.com shows hundreds of genres and thousands of "programs"— though there is no way to know how often individual podcasters upload programs. Since podcasts come to listeners through subscription services as well as through individual downloads, there is no accurate measure of whether the downloads are actually heard, but Bridge estimates that by 2010, there will be a potential audience of at least 45 million.[22] With this figure in mind, mainstream broadcasters and other media outlets have taken it on themselves to get into the business sooner, rather than later.

IS THIS POLITICAL PARTICIPATION?

When the electorate is informed, political participation is enhanced, but not necessarily guaranteed. While it may be true that more information is better than a little information or biased information, no amount of information alone can motivate anyone to vote, run for office, or participate in governance. When more information is available, the battlefield between and among ideological viewpoints is delineated. Controversies over whether news media present biased information or not has been of critical importance to the effective maintenance of democracy. Many citizen watchdog groups exist, such as Fairness and Accuracy in Reporting

(FAIR) and the Citizens Internet Empowerment Coalition (CIEC), as well as others, to keep tabs on media industry activities, and questions of bias have shifted over the years. Before deregulation and media conglomeration, the usual claim was that the media were too liberal; after deregulation, with the ascendancy of Fox Broadcasting and the Christian Broadcasting Network, many claim that the media now are too conservative. If big media can be proven to have a bias, or an individual feels that a program or network has a bias, the Internet and bloggers offer a much broader range of political opinions from which to choose. This is not the real issue, though. What is more important is the way the audience thinks of the validity of the information on the Internet, and if the Internet becomes a trusted friend and personal medium, it is much more likely to be viewed in a favorable light.

NEWS OF WAR

Coverage of war has always been subject to a number of problems for the journalist who covers the conflict, as well as for government and military personnel who would like to control the type of information that becomes public. The Bush administration requested that all major media broadcasters refrain from broadcasting images of soldiers killed in Iraq; pictures of flag-draped caskets, grieving widows, or even maimed servicemen are generally not covered by mainstream media. But blogs can do much more. Bloggers within Iraq have told their stories in very human, very painful terms. Soldiers can keep blogs that can be accessed by their families (though soldiers are asked to restrict information about their whereabouts, or any military actions), and many blogs exist to give audiences information that the mainstream press will not give, such as the number of Americans killed in service or the number of Iraqis killed in the War in Iraq. For those who crave this information, it is important that there is an outlet for it. Yahoo! hired the experienced ABC journalist Kevin Sites to be a one-man production team of journalist, cameraman, and operations manager, sending stories to Yahoo! via his computer and a satellite-based cell phone.[23]

Some of the most powerful information about the reality of the War in Iraq come from soldiers' blogs that tell of the human side of warfare. John Hockenberry writes about what he refers to as *milbloggers* (military bloggers), who he says "constitute a rich subculture with a refreshing candor about the war, expressing views ranging from far right to far left."[24] Their blogs, along with those of Iraqi citizens and others who are passionate about the American involvement in Iraq, have provided a rich cultural text that would not have been available but for the instant, open access of the Internet. But it is also the openness to postings that could potentially challenge the way the Internet operates today, if governments crack down on personal information that might be deemed a security risk.

Certainly blogging and podcasting show that it is possible for more individuals to put their ideas on the Internet. For those who make their sites "official" looking and authoritative, there is a chance that the growing number of people who use these services can use them as sources of news and information. The problem with this is that so many individuals can't tell the difference between a professionally produced blog or podcast that was put up by an individual and one that was posted by an organization that has checked the facts, attempted to explore the issue from many sides, and taken journalistic care to present the material in such a way as to prevent the reader/user from absorbing any bias. As technology gets cheaper, more amateurs can make their sites look professional, but what they may be espousing is opinion rather than fact. The timeliness of information on the Internet does a lot to lead people to believe that it is a superior medium to traditional media, and the personal nature of using the computer in an intimate setting strengthens the dependence on the technology to provide "all the news there is." But, as indicated, too much information can overwhelm someone, and in the act of being selective, it is most likely that the person will browse longer on sites that confirm or reaffirm his or her own attitudes and biases.

Added to this is the problem that arises when a medium is successful. The commercialization of the Internet has unwittingly invited either those who are entrepreneurial or those who just hope to make a fast buck. Because blogs are user generated and can link to other pages or blogs, the phenomenon of *splogging*, or spamming blogs, has also flooded the Internet.[25] Although those in the profession of creating splogs prefer to call their businesses "search engine marketers" and claim the same rights as any blogger who capitalizes on the freedom of expression afforded by the Internet, splogs are get-rich-quick schemes that build advertising into phoney blog pages and entice people (especially the heavy users, viz. Internet addicts, gamers, and shoppers) to click on ads that run next to text, or link to a Web site that sidetracks the people accessing information from their site. Since search companies such as Google, Yahoo!, and MSN all receive revenue for the number of clicks on those ads (as well as advertisers), search engines are unlikely to censor these types of blogs, though the integrity of running them has forced some to look into ways of curbing their number. What is at stake is the openness of Web 2.0, which is the architecture that allows anyone to post information. This growing commercializm annoys many consumers and leads to sensory overload. The consequences of this open architecture is what makes the Internet vulnerable to so many problems, and the amount of spam is a leading reason for some people to become "don't wants" in the world of the Internet.

The threat is very real. As Charles C. Mann writes, "People in the industry disagree about how to beat back spam, or whether it can even be done. But there's no dispute that if the blogosphere and the rest of Web 2.0 can't find a way to stop the sleaze-balls who are enveloping the Net in a haze of babble and cheesy marketing, then the best features of Web 2.0 will be turned off."[26] While the demise of the Internet as we know it has been a matter of concern for many, several organizations have already staked a claim to maintain the open architecture and fight for legislation to legitimize access to the Internet. The Electronic Freedom Forum (EFF) is one example of such an organization, and activists have begun to lobby Congress to guarantee the same rights to bloggers as those given to journalists. The EFF has actively become involved in establishing rights for bloggers to exercise free speech, monitor and participate in political speech, and protect bloggers' anonymity.[27]

The efforts of the EFF and other groups have been somewhat successful. In 2006, the Federal Election Commission endorsed the position that bloggers should be allowed to engage in political activity on the Internet, with the only exception that they may not be paid for political endorsements.[28] In addition to bloggers' views on political issues and their criticism and commentary, the Internet has proven to be an effective means of changing political fund-raising for specific candidates and of reaching younger news and public affairs consumers to interest them in political issues.

In addition to blogs, the Internet does allow individuals who are interested in specific candidates to do research on the candidates' views and to share ideas with the candidates and political parties through e-mail. In this way, the Internet acts as an electronic town hall, expanding the possibility of getting questions and comments to candidates either for election purposes or for the routine maintenance of political processes in civic life. When this happens, the positive aspects of the Internet are also underscored. The possibility for electronic dialogue capitalizes on the instantaneous ability to send and receive messages and can have enormous implications for politicians to understand their constituency's needs and desires. As a medium for mobilizing information for those interested, the Internet can provide direct access to politicians, officials, and those committed to political processes.

CELL PHONES AND POLITICAL PARTICIPATION

Telephones as direct connections to the home have long been used in political campaigns to encourage voters to vote and for polling purposes. Computerized messages from candidates, called *robo calls* because they are made from an automatic dialer, have increased over the years as a way of trying to make a somewhat personal connection with individuals or those in a household. Along with increases in direct-marketing practices, robo calls are one more way of trying to mobilize individuals to action in an attempt to make a personal, albeit mediated, connection to someone. Unless an unethical practice on the Internet results in spam that advocates the message of a politician or a special-interest group, the Internet remains a technology in which the individual user must choose to access information. The telephone, though, is still thought of as a more direct connection into the home. Even if a person is not taking a call, answering machines can record messages, and politicians hope that any part of a message heard will reinforce a name or position.

While it may take a while to understand the potential for cell phones to affect the political process in America, there has already been one major shift in how cell phones might be used to help shape the agenda for social and political change. Will Lester wrote that in the 2006 elections, pollsters, who have long relied on contacting individuals through their wired phones, might undergo change in the future as more people rely on cell phones only.[29] Both Republican and Democratic grassroots campaigners also used cell phones to sponsor *calling parties* during the 2006 election, where political activists gathered in someone's home and used cell phones for the purpose of calling many different people at the same time to encourage them to vote.

Though cell phones are just becoming tools to enhance some aspects of political participation, the Internet has already become a powerful medium for the expression of diverse viewpoints that the mainstream media no longer present. The future of more highly converged technologies, especially the potential for voting over the Internet or for using cell phones with greater Internet access, could present the American public with many additional options for understanding political issues and becoming more involved in political processes.

Will the personal communication characteristics of cell phones and the Internet grow in ways that enhance democratic participation? Traditional media are undergoing regulatory and content changes, and the Internet has already opened opportunities for people to gain access to more information—if they chose to seek it. Understanding how individuals view themselves as part of society is important for democracy, but does this draw on the more personal characteristics of these technologies? In the emerging world of cell phones and using the Internet for a greater number of purposes, many things are still unknown, but one thing is certain. Many aspects of our culture are likely to undergo a greater change, and cell phones and the Internet will undoubtedly be used to facilitate this change.

Six

Social Spaces and Scary Places

As the previous chapters have demonstrated, both cell phones and the Internet are often used as personal technologies and can be thought of in very intimate terms by their users. These qualities can enhance social relationships and provide some satisfying experiences for users unless they allow the technology to take control of personal time. But sometimes, depending on the needs of the person using the technology, the users may be disappointed with the quality of the interaction. After all, when a machine comes between two people, there is no physical *body* in the relationship. There may be a certain amount of vicarious pleasure and sense of "connection" with another human being, but mediated interaction is still a substitute for real, personal, physical intimacy or even the experience of face-to-face communication. Depending on the person's needs, the desire to make human connections through technology and the expectation for intimacy and privacy—especially through the Internet—can be disappointing and possibly alienating.

This chapter addresses the personal uses of *social networking* programs on the Internet and explores how people use socially constructed spaces to meet like-minded people, make friends, and possibly cultivate romance. These examples are indicators of how the Internet provides an outlet for social interaction, even in situations where face-to-face communication could be produce anxiety. Social networking raises the question of whether relationships can be established and maintained online and whether these types of social interactions are as fulfilling as face-to-face interactions when people express themselves in intimate terms, over a form of media. The chapter also addresses the changes in personal conversation that both the Internet and cell phones facilitate and the ways in which this type of communication affects social relationships. These new practices and behaviors indicate how our culture is responding to new ways of communicating from a very personal perspective.

When used privately and for emotional purposes, both cell phones and the Internet allow the person to divulge deep, personal desires and information. Opening up to someone over a form of media can be very helpful to someone who doesn't have many social opportunities or who may experience social anxiety, and a mediated relationship is still better than not having any contact with others at all, but the personal use of technology can also result in a loss of personal privacy. In the case of cell phones and the Internet, the loss of *control* over one's privacy can result in a whole host of problems, including spam, phishing, and ultimately, identity, and it can lead toward new attitudes about privacy and the role of government regulations and policies that establish guidelines for the security of private information. The dangers associated with using these technologies for human interactions where trust in others is assumed, but not guaranteed, shows some of the potential problems with using digital technology for intimate, personal reasons, and reaffirms the possibility that the more technologies we have to communicate, the less we really may communicate.

PEOPLE WHO NEED PEOPLE

Everyone knows that the need for close personal relationships is part of being human. Physical attraction, emotional bonding, and personal connection to other people is a key ingredient for human happiness, and a sense of belonging to family and peer groups, and the ability to love and be loved, is critical to the psychological and social balance for all human beings. So wouldn't it make sense to assume that technologies that are, by their very nature, capable of facilitating and enhancing social relationships—a benefit for people? Several attempts have been made to use technologies to foster personal relationships in the past decades to address this challenge.

In the 1960s, several commercial services became available to consumers, promising that computers and scientific methods could be used to help people make social connections and find satisfying relationships. Surveys helped identify what a person was looking for in another individual in terms of friendship, companionship, or the desire for a long-term relationship. The surveys charted personal habits and values, which were then coded on punch cards and processed by computer. There, the technology, unencumbered by social anxiety, shyness, or fear, could dispassionately sort the information and provide a list of possible matches with people of similar interests and values. At first the idea seemed to be a novelty, but by the 1970s, the number of "matchmaker" services and companies were so successful that newspapers and magazines began to offer "personals" to participate in the relationship industry. The anonymity afforded someone who placed a personal ad in the paper might have encouraged many people to try making contacts in a low-risk manner, but they also fueled the media's portrayal of the typical personal ad reader as someone who led a lonely, singles' life during the days of disco fever and personal anomie. The lonely life of the unattached single man or woman was characterized as one of the unpleasant attributes of a society in which work overshadowed issues of the quality of personal life. The late Boomers were particularly vulnerable, having spent more time on developing professional careers that limited social time with others. With the "loneliness industry" firmly in place by the mid-1970s, computer dating services, personal ads, and professional relationship consultants began to flourish. The consumers for most of these services were not the younger segment of the population, as might be expected. They were people in their thirties and forties who had spent much of their time establishing their careers. The "typical" client for computer dating services was a professional who had little time to attend social gatherings, where they might meet others. Clients for personal ads in print media tended to be those who had less disposable income to hire a dating service, or those who experienced so much social anxiety that they felt compelled to start "relationships" by phone or mail.

Also in the 1970s, the development of the offset printing press reduced the cost for publishing special-interest magazines and newspapers. Persons with particular interests, like finding a same-sex partner, or those who had other common interests, sexually or otherwise, found it possible to submit personals to these publications that would be more likely to attract the attention of willing, like-minded people.

As home computers began to come onto the market in the 1980s, Internet service providers began to offer chat rooms, bulletin boards, and other personal services that capitalized on the ability of the computer and Internet to make social connections with others. The fact that users could access these services from the comfort and security of their private homes helped enormously in treating these services as private, personal communications. The growing epidemic of HIV and AIDS, and the media's attention to the spread of the disease, contributed to driving some types of social interaction away from public places and toward more private venues.

With greater commercialization of services available on the Internet in the 1990s, "social networking" sites began to gain attention. The term was coined in the early 2000s to describe software that can facilitate personal interaction over networks. While businesses often establish in-house sites specifically to encourage collaborative work, the term is usually used to describe the hundreds of services that are available for two purposes: for online dating and relationship issues and for participation in virtual communities. In each case the Internet extends a sense of a designated *space* for a form of social interaction to take place. While social networking sites can be used for a variety of reasons, the most common purpose is for either cultivating friends or romantic relationships, or participating in sexual fantasies—all from the convenience, comfort, and privacy of your home, with your computer connected to the Internet. In the area of making friends or having a romantic relationship, social networks are perfect examples of how what once was a public activity (meeting people) has become a private activity. In the case of sexual fantasy, social networking demonstrates how what has usually been a private action or thought now enters another dimension in cyberspace.

CLICK HERE FOR ROMANCE

Is there anyone these days who doesn't know someone who has had a relationship with someone they met over the Internet? Even if the relationship isn't intimate, the Internet allows us to meet others and establish some type of emotional response with others, whether they are colleagues or old friends. Is seems only natural that commercial services would attempt to capitalize on the relationship-building features of Internet services.

The first commercial site to offer a dating/mating service went online in 1995, with the name Match.com. This 24/7 Internet service promises to identify potential users in a number of ways, by special interest, physical description, religion, location, drinking habits, and a host of other traits, and presents new users with a checklist of what they desire in others, as well as how they describe themselves. Within a short time after hitting the Internet, more than 500 users a day were registering for the site.

Soon other sites went online, such as eHarmony, PerfectMatch.com, and Chemistry.com, just to name a few of the hundreds that now exist. All of these services promise a scientific approach to understanding romantic compatibility as a component of finding a long-lasting love. In the words of the journalist Lori Gottlieb, "Collectively, their efforts mark the early days of a social experiment of unprecedented proportions, involving millions of couples and possibly extending over the course of generations. The question at the heart of this grand trial is simple: In the subjective realm of love, can cold, hard science help?"[1] While each of the major online services measures compatibility, personality, and other traits, each boasts of success on the basis of the number of successful matches it makes, and each has different methods of evaluating client compatibility. eHarmony, for example, uses a 436-item questionnaire, reportedly searching for the categories that would predict long-term compatibility. Between September 2004 and September 2005, eHarmony claimed to have facilitated the marriages of more than 33,000 members. Furthermore, according to an in-house study of almost 300 married couples, the relationships were reported to be more satisfactory than those made by more conventional meeting, dating, and courtship activities.[2] In a more objective study, in 2005, the Pew Internet and American Life Project conducted a survey of over 3,000 individuals to assess online dating habits. They found that of the single people looking for partners, 37 percent claimed to have tried online sites; of those, about half had actually gone on dates as a result of their online search, and about one-third formed long-term relationships.[3]

While the statistics compiled by commercial ventures seem to point to an impressive number of satisfied and successful matches, the Pew Internet and American Life data suggest that perhaps the phenomenon of using online services to find romance may not be as successful as the commercial services claim. This is no surprise, but the data suggest a number of different issues regarding who is likely to use these services and what happens when they use them. Several studies have shown that the desired needs of users markedly shape their satisfaction and reasons for participating in online relationships. Some commercial online dating services have some features that are "free" to potential users, but most charge a fee for their expanded services, limiting their availability to those who can afford them or those who feel these services to be so important that they are willing to make the financial commitment to take advantage of them. Most of the users of online dating/romance subscribers are people for whom time is an important factor. These people, too, are likely to be Boomers who have had decades of familiarity with personals in print media, and for whom there may be no stigma attached to trying something new in the arena of computer help for finding and making relationships. But while commercial services may boast of using scientific methods and trained "matchmakers" to facilitate interactions with clients, it is interesting to think about how the noncommercial services offer potential matches to their users.

Search engines such as Yahoo! and Google offer free personal chat rooms that expand the range of meeting people online to a broader potential audience, many of whom don't necessarily seek romance, but who do want to make friends or find companionship over the Internet. In a survey, Dore Hollander found that among the respondents between the ages of eighteen and twenty-four, partners were usually found in chat rooms rather than on commercial sites. For this group, more than 40 percent reported having sex with a partner they met over the Internet. Even more surprisingly, two-thirds of the respondents in this group reported that partners they had met over the Internet had lied about their age, and more than a third said they had met someone who had lied about his or her marital status.[4]

Overwhelmingly, online dating and matchmaking services seem to appeal to people who have little time to socialize outside the home or work or those who suffer some form of social anxiety that makes it difficult for them to relate to others in a face-to-face setting. Using the features of the anonymity afforded by social networking, persons can identify themselves in words, rather than feeling exposed and vulnerable to other peoples' immediate face-to-face reaction to them. In today's world, where so many people feel that their bodies don't measure up to supermodels, body builders, or people with flawless physical features, getting to know someone through the expression of private thoughts can help someone feel far less vulnerable to rejection. Many people feel more confident when they can communicate over distance, without risking the social anxiety of having to meet someone face-to-face, and fears of embarrassment or rejection are initially reduced when the risk of personal rejection is low.

Everyone probably knows someone who has posted a picture on one of the Internet social networking sites that was taken many years earlier, when the person was thinner and younger and perhaps had more hair, but by and large, when a physical meeting takes place after an initial attraction from one of these types of pictures, the relationship is usually doomed. This leads to yet another feature of Internet communication: misrepresentation, or outright lying that often occurs when people can choose anonymity or represent themselves as someone or something else other than who they are.

Beatriz Lia and Avila Mileham write that people who participate in Internet chat rooms can have sexual relationships in cyberspace, while still being married or in a long-term relationship with a physical partner.[5] They characterizes three types of online identity formations, including "anonymous sexual interactionism," which takes place when the individual is seeking anonymous sexual gratification in a chat room; "behavioral rationalization," which shows how people tell themselves that having an online sexual relationship is innocent and harmless; and "effortless avoidance," which is the users' avoidance of any psychological discomfort that would come from a real-world sexual activity. Sexuality and identity are key issues to how people think of themselves when they participate in a social network. "Cybersexuality" which occurs online, but not in the real world, is a sexual space that is "midway between fantasy and action"[6]

USING AND ABUSING SOCIAL NETWORKS

Personal experience and the need for interaction are key factors for anyone who engages in social networking, and they are the predictors of satisfaction with online relationships. Certainly anyone can be more vulnerable than usual at certain times in life, especially after a romantic breakup, loss of a loved one, or some other personal trauma, and in this case, the ability of an online relationship to present a connection to someone at a distance can allow relationships to grow over time that can be comforting and helpful. But another nagging feature invades our lives daily and affects some users' attitudes toward social networks and online dating: synchronous, real-world time. At the same time, a belief in what romance is and does plays an enormous role in whether someone will be satisfied with online relationships.

In the Pew Internet and American Life Project (Table 3.3), older users appeared to find social networking a comfort and engaged in a moderate amount of online communication, though the data don't represent whether the relationships are with family, friends, or strangers. If the Matures use these services for romance, more power to them! For those who may be house bound or have limited mobility, the social aspects of the Internet can be very important. For many, what constitutes a sense of romance or companionship influences the satisfaction levels of those who seek long-term relationships.

In an experimental study, Andrea Bergstrom surveyed a select group of individuals who had used online dating services, and found that most did so because they felt they had limited opportunities to meet new people in their daily lives. As one of her Boomer respondents reported,

> At any age it is difficult to meet people—but I feel it's harder in middle age. If you don't meet at work, then options are more limited. Most clubs, sports bars, any of those sorts of places are geared to a younger crowd. With Internet dating, you can read many profiles and narrow down people to those who have interests in common with you. You can send email, communicate anonymously, with no risk of hurting anyone, or being hurt. In middle age most people you meet are married or in a relationship, or have way too much baggage. By using the net you can get a feel for whether or not you are interested in getting to someone without having invested a lot of energy or time.[7]

Bergstrom found that physical attractiveness in pictures posted on the Internet was a key determinant of how her subjects made decisions about whom to contact, leading her to surmise, "Consistently, even though the participants wanted to avoid personal judgments from others in regard to their own appearances . . . the participants themselves often still based their decisions about talking to and meeting potential dates on the physical appearances revealed in one or two pictures posted in a profile."[8] For these participants, the Internet facilitated meeting someone, but the criteria for attraction were still based on physical appearance.

As might be expected, younger users have found their own ways to make sense of social networking sites, and for them, romance is not necessarily a key feature. Daniel Knox, Lakisha Sturdivant, and Marty E. Zusman[9] conducted a survey of 191 college students and found that over 40 percent of the respondents sought new friends over the Internet, rather than a romantic partner. Half of the respondents used the online services because they wanted to reduce the anxiety of a face-to-face encounter. Of that group, 60 percent reported that they physically met someone they had initially met online, and that about one-fourth of these meetings resulted in friendships.

Users from generations C and Y tend to draw on different types of social networking programs, such as *Friendster, MySpace*, or *Facebook*, all of which target the college-age audience, or even those who are younger, though MySpace, in particular, has been the fastest-growing social networking site, with over 75 million users ranging from teenagers to Matures.[10] MySpace is a bit of an anomaly in the world of social networking because it also tends to lead toward using the social networking apparatus for the posting of video projects that are made by individuals and posted to the Internet, with opportunities to comment and vote on the creativity and likability of certain videos. Like blogging, MySpace can distribute very specific content that expresses creativity, in addition to being used for social networking purposes.

When people use one of the more traditionally "pure" social networking sites such as Friendster or Facebook, they post personal information that describes how they feel and what they like, and often a number of pictures that project the image they want to convey to others. These sites don't necessarily exist for purposes of creating romance or looking for partners, but they do capitalize on the desire for people to meet others who have similar interests and qualities.

Facebook in particular has the purpose of trying to help students on college campuses meet and expand their range of friends. In 2002, Harvard students Mark Zuckerberg, Tyler and Cameron Winklevoss, and Divya Narendra all worked on a social networking program called HarvardConnection to help students on the Harvard campus post a bit of personal information and a picture or two in order to help identify students on campus. By February 2004, Zuckerberg and a couple of friends had developed Thefacebook.com, which they posted on "a normal night in the dorm." Within twenty-four hours, approximately 1,200 to 1,500 registrants had signed up for the program, and a new phenomenon had been born. Quickly, the site became a place for self-promotion as well as a source of creating social interaction.[11] Zuckerberg gained financial control over the site and marketed it to other campuses, but because the location was fixed and tied to a particular campus, the range of people to meet and the type of information available were restricted to those who were on a particular campus.

MySpace and Friendster are examples of social networking sites that are available to anyone, and as a result, they have often been subject to greater misuse by others who exploit the features of the Internet. Because of people's ability to lie, post information anonymously, or locate someone (who might not want to be found), these services are resulting in a host of new questions about privacy and trust on the Internet.

Some of the most dangerous features about posting any personal information on the Internet reflect matters of trust that someone has when using a service, and the control they use or lose when they post that information. Children and young adults are among the most trusting users of the Internet, and by now, we know that they are also the most likely to post personal information, feeling that the personal, intimate nature of the Internet is a positive feature, rather than one that can be abused by others. Parents have been concerned that their children might come across messages posted by pedophiles, whose goals are to influence or harm the young users,[12] a reality that has become only too common in recent years. Many teens or college students feel that they control their personal space and post less-than-flattering pictures of themselves, sometimes showing them drunk, lewd, or represented by images or words that might be embarrassing to them if their parents or possible employers saw them. What these social networking participants forget is that once digital information goes online, anyone can find it. This has resulted in a growing number of employers who have used social networking to research a potential job candidate's suitability for a position,[13] and raising ethical questions about law enforcement monitoring of sites and using information from social networking sites as material for journalists. At the *Seattle Times* a reporter accessed the MySpace page for a suspect who had killed four people and set fire to their home, only to find a self-disclosed record of how the alleged suspect had dealt with his history of drug abuse and alcohol, and a picture he had posted, which then was used in the *Times* news story.[14]

Since so many students use social networking sites, schools have begun to offer guidelines on how students should behave and what type of etiquette is appropriate for social networking behavior. Most guidelines remind students that it's not always a good idea to post pictures of themselves in embarrassing situations, and ask students to be aware of what might be considered friendly behavior as opposed to weird behavior. Students are warned that browsing profiles for hours can classify someone as a stalker, without actually calling attention to the possibility of Internet addiction. Most importantly, they try to prevent students from trashing other people's profiles, commenting on their physical attributes, and lying about their current relationship status.

There is also one other interesting feature of using social networking for building connections among friends, and it has to do with the emerging protocol for how to remove someone from your list of friends on a social network. Many people have felt hurt or powerless when all of a sudden they have been "de-friended" by someone on their friend list. If the friend was actually someone known in the real world, the result can be as devastating to someone as getting dumped by a lover, or snubbed by one of your peers. The awkward interaction that results when the parties see each other in a face-to-face environment can be uncomfortable for both of the individuals.

PRIVACY AND PERSONAL INFORMATION

Social networking is just one type of Internet service that exacts a level of trust and thrives on personal disclosure of information. When this becomes a normal activity for people, eventually, over time, attitudes toward privacy begin to change. Simson Garfinkle writes in *Database Nation: The Death of Privacy in the 21st Century*, "Over the next 50 years, we will see new kinds of threats to privacy that don't find their roots in totalitarianism, but in capitalism, the free market, advanced technology, and the unbridled exchange of electronic information."[15] The range of information available over the Internet is *virtually limitless*, and those words are used to be intentionally descriptive. Space on the Internet is virtual; we can't see it or touch it, but we know that the amount of information available to us is quite truly limitless, if we know how to access it. Because computers have features that mask the way computers and the Internet work together, a good deal of information remains stored in places that we can't easily see or even comprehend. Offering personal information while thinking that we are connected directly to someone is one thing, but because of the architecture of the Internet and the storage capacity of the computers or cell phones that we use, a vast amount of stored data is available to anyone who knows how to access it. What this means is that digital information is highly vulnerable to hackers. A company can unobtrusively plant a *cookie* to a hard drive that acts as a mediator of our personal use of the computer and the company that embeds the cookie into the software we use. Digital systems make us vulnerable to the software designs of others that are obvious when we receive spam or unwanted ads. Unless we periodically clean up the cookies or use filters, firewalls, or antivirus software, we don't even know when our hard drives—those little exsosomatic memories full of personal information about us and our habits—are tapped into for unethical purposes. This is one of the great ironies of using digital technology; we think we have greater personal control over the technology, but we do become vulnerable to others when someone else invades our computers or cell phones to use our own information to harm us. Once again, the illusion of control sometimes results in violation of our personal data.

Search engines such as Google and Yahoo! collect an extraordinary amount of information about people, including what they access, how long they stay online, and whom they contact. In writing about Google, Adam Penenberg states, "The question is . . . whether Google, with its insatiable thirst for your personal data, has become the greatest threat to privacy ever known, a vast informational honey pot that attracts hackers, crackers, online thieves, and—perhaps most worrisome of all—a government intent on finding convenient ways to spy on its own citizenry."[16] Although Penenberg cites Google's claim that it has never erased any data in its history, the image of how much information Google might actually possess calls forth the image of Big Brother, identified by George Orwell in his book *1984*. Although search engines do have massive amounts of data from interactions by users, more common threats come from smaller hackers and professional thieves intent on causing trouble, harming your data, or harvesting information for their own use. Identity theft is just one of the many problems that can result from these insidious practices, but the mining of data by organizations intent on using personal information for profit has also resulted in big business, as well as problems for law enforcement and the legal system.

Phishing is a typical tactic to tempt people to willingly give personal information away to thieves. Clever robbers or companies that use our information for unethical purposes prey on our belief that the Internet is used for personal purposes and that the network is trustworthy. The typical phishing scheme looks so professional that Internet users think they are working with bona fide information from a source. Messages from banks, the IRS, or any type of organization that might ask you to give some personal information (social security number, account numbers, passwords, etc.) masquerade as professional inquiries, but often result in a person willingly submitting personal information to a professional thief. During one month in 2006, the number of unique phishing sites, those specifically designed to attack personal information stored on a person's computer and accessible by the Internet, and information stored on cell phones, increased by 55 percent.[17]

Cell phones are also not immune from these problems. Not only can a regular call be overheard and used by someone for a nefarious reason (which is why we should never give a credit card number over a cell phone in a public place), but the features on cell phones with great functionality can be just as much of a target for information thieves as a personal computer.[18] As cell phones begin to be used more for Internet access, they, too, can be easily hacked, and the information stored on them abused as well. Phone number directories, calendar appointments, and cloning numbers that come into a person's cell phones are common targets of cell phone hackers.

Adware and spyware are also problems that affect both computers and cell phones. Adware is a type of software system that reports back to an advertising company about the sites that people visit online. Spyware not only does the same thing as adware, but also it can transfer data to hackers, who can use the information for identity theft or other illegal purposes. All of these areas fall into the category of cybercrime and present problems for law enforcement professionals because they are so hard to trace in multidimensional cyberspace.

The rise in cybercrime has also resulted in a number of new products designed to help keep personal information just that—personal. The protection of privacy has become big business, resulting in a proliferation of companies that develop, market, and sell devices to protect privacy on the Internet, cell phones, and for home and business securitiy.[19] As people purchase and use new software systems and virus suites (services that assure a range of content protection systems) to assure themselves of some level of control, we also give up some traditional notions of privacy and security. What happens, too, is that the greater number of devices we buy and use, the more we cross traditional boundaries of safety and security, and privacy and surveillance.

For many years, veterinarians have offered the service of implanting a small chip under a pet's skin. If the animal strays or is lost, any veterinarian can read the code and reunite the pet with its owner. Today, though, the idea of implanting chips in children, either under their skin, or in a device given them, such as a cell phone with a location tracker, is becoming more common. While many people are appalled at chipping or tagging children, the idea of using a simple, harmless technology to identify their whereabouts seems less problematic for many. The wireless umbilical cord maintains the illusion of control. Even if the idea of tagging children seems distasteful, cell phones have offered the same type of service. The Disney Company markets a cell phone specifically for this purpose.[20] The Disney phone is complete with a GPS tracking system that allows a parent to know where the child is, even when the child is not speaking on the phone. These particular phones are programmed to call only certain numbers, such as the home or the parents' offices or cell phones. If a parent also has a Disney phone, he or she can monitor the child's whereabouts; if not, she or he can track the child through a service on the Internet. On the surface, these phones can be marketed in all good faith and with the express purpose of safety—which few people could claim is a social problem. But at the same time, this type of phone is emblematic of the way small technologies can begin to lead us to different expectations of control, the illusion of control, and very likely, the ultimate sacrifice of control as we willingly reconceptualize values of privacy and independence.

Of course, trying to make such a claim about young children is weak. Safety needs must prevail, and we would hasten to chastise the parents who didn't attempt to exercise their parental responsibility over young children. At the same time, these youngsters grow up with a different attitude and expectation of who knows where they are, and they expect to have their actions monitored. It is then a short step away from parents monitoring their children to the government creating laws and using tactics to monitor the whereabouts of all citizens. The end result is that our technologies seem harmless, but can potentially change the entire social system of privacy and surveillance.

CELL SPEAK AND NO SPEAK

Conversation has long been thought to reflect the type of social environment that establishes rules for speech. Traditionally we reserve some types of speech for professional areas, some types for social speech with our friends and family, and even more intimate types for special personal relationships. Particular styles of speech may exist between husband and wife, parent and child, or lovers. These different types of speech are also defined by the way people feel comfortable talking when they are in different places. Conversations in public are usually different than those in private. For this reason, when someone uses a cell phone in a public place for personal reasons, the conversation may seem out of place.

Cell phones do much more than annoy us in public places by unwanted ringing and our inability to avoid unwanted, inappropriate eavesdropping. They are contributing to the changing nature of conversation. While the early users of the fixed-wire telephone had to be coached to greet a caller with a simple protocol or pleasantry like "hello," cell phones have become so personal that users often don't bother with traditional greetings. Perhaps this is a function of having a readout of who is calling, but the typical cell phone user now is not even conscious of answering the phone with declarative sentences, and identifying a caller by name. This is an illustration of how the technology easily leads us to change behavior.

Of course, one reason why people often speak louder on cell phones than they would on a wired phone is that the quality of the cell phone call is often poor. If a cell phone signal is weak, the person at one end tends to overcompensate by raising the voice, too. Using the phones in public places also means that often the hubbub of restaurants, train stations, or store traffic is in the background, thus prompting the person on the phone to shout to overcome the environmental disturbance.

These people may not intentionally be acting obnoxiously—they may just be trying to be heard. But still, their behavior easily annoys everyone around them.

Cell phone users also use the immediacy factor of the cell phone to usher in a type of conversation that is characterized by fragmented sentences, emphasizing more declarative statements than a reciprocal conversation would (often, this is because so many people leave messages when they can't access their conversation partners in synchronous time). In a *Boston Globe Magazine* article, John Powers wrote about contemporary conversation that has been reduced to shorthand in both words and images. He demonstrated how we've begun to speak in a "code" that reflects real-time communication that is influenced by the immediacy of the technology, and he said that the shorthand "values not only simplicity over complexity, but reaction over reflection."[21] When texting and using abbreviations for words, the cell speak becomes even more cryptic and less communicative. As these new languages emerge, the art of traditional conversation begins to undergo greater change. Once we had a very formal style of expression, which has become far more informal over the years. Will the types of cryptic comments used in e-mail or text messaging enter into our conversation? They've already begun to infiltrate the way people think, so it's likely that shorthand conversational style will change to accommodate those messages, especially for social speech.

It may also seem strange that when we use the Internet to communicate with others, we have no reference to voice, accent, speech impediment, or even timbre. The image of others with whom we interact only over e-mail or an Internet service is an image that takes place in our own minds. We might imagine physical characteristics from the style of presentation, but unless we hear the voice, we lose the ability to sense many qualities about the people with whom we interact. Even when we see a picture of someone, we can't relate to the body language or any gestures that communicate so much impact and emotion, when we remove ourselves from the aural/oral world. This in itself isn't necessarily bad; in fact, many people would claim that the type of interaction that isn't based on sensory impression might be a clearer understanding of the other person's mind; but whatever the position, the interaction takes on a different nature than face-to-face communication.

FROM ONLINE ROMANCE TO CHANGING CONVERSATIONS

Many people have attempted to supplement their lives with services on the Internet and cell phones. For those who expect these technologies to radically transform their lives by increasing the number of friends or romantic partners they meet, these technologies seem, on the surface, to have what it takes to facilitate interaction. But at the same time, they have qualities that make individuals far more vulnerable to the loss of their own private information and lead them to think that the solution to technological problems is to have more technology. The good and bad features of the Internet and cell phones are intertwined, but until people negotiate appropriate ways to use these technologies, we can expect to see more abuse by those who are intent on causing harm or profiting by others' losses.

Although conversation may be more spontaneous, the messages are more fragmented than in traditional conversation. Privacy is becoming more of a problem for people who use these technologies, because many thieves see these tools as moneymaking opportunities. As data become valuable, our society needs to collectively decide who owns personal information and what penalties might be appropriate for punishing those who betray the trust a person has when using technology for personal reasons. The evidence of social change seems clear, but the solutions will be a long time coming. With these cultural aspects of cell phone and Internet use in mind, we move to a better understanding of what we know and what type of control we do have over the ownership of our personal information.

Bites and Fragments: What Do We Know?
What Do We Own?

When people use cell phones and the Internet without considering the possible negative consequences, like losing control over personal information, they fail to see some of the inevitable repercussions of relying on technology. When they fail to understand how some of the more subtle social changes occur, such as the way we speak or maintain personal social relationships, they also lose sight of how our social patterns are changing. When the combination of technical forces, assumptions about the integrity of the technology, and human needs come together, the result can be a naive reliance on information that is easily consumed, but not critically questioned. The social evidence points to the problem of a growing tendency for people to think less, react more quickly, and rush to judgment that might be more instinctual than thoughtful. The combination of forces that encompass matters of time (technologically controlled time, human beings' use of time, and the assumptions about taking information at face value), show how our society is affected by *fragmented* thinking that challenges the individual to ponder the contexts and consequences for how they use the media and information presented to them by digital technologies.

Certainly when people converse on a cell phone, use text messaging, or establish a social relationship with someone over the Internet whom they've never met or seen, the satisfaction with the interaction is in part defined by the whether the individuals involved feel that their personal needs for communication are fulfilled. But when people reach data bases for other types of information, time pressures often result in shortcuts that affect the quality of the information accessed. When people trust information on the Internet, they may not be critically evaluating whether the information is an opinion blog or a commercial splog, or whether they're being tempted to respond to a phishing scam. All information on the Internet is not equal; it comes with the same range of biases, slant, interpretation, and sales pitches that we see in all other forms of media. But because some of the services on the Internet appear to be so trustworthy, it is easy to want to rely on those sources as matters of *fact* rather than opinion or for commercial purposes. The nature of what we know is highly influenced by the characteristics of the Internet as a source of information, and the way we think of the Internet in personal, intimate ways. As cell phones become more functional and can access the Internet, they too can be tools for finding information that can be misleading, or wrong.

Instant access to information on the Internet has led more people to view the Internet as an all-knowing Oracle of information. There is so much information that *is* valid and is presented so professionally that when presented on a visual screen, the information *looks* authoritative. Online versions of trusted newspapers and magazines carry with them the authority of traditional print converted to an electronic form. The ability to access libraries of data and official websites also carry the imprimatur of trust and validity. But trouble can follow when the sites posted by individuals, corporations, or scam artists are creatively presented to resemble factual information. As different types of content posted by people with a variety of motivations flood the Internet, two important aspects of thinking about information are called into question. The first aspect is whether it is possible to judge the trustworthiness or validity of the information; the second is the question of who owns the information. These two questions are unmistakably linked in the quest to understand the impact of both cell phones and the Internet on American culture.

There is a tremendous irony in the linking of these two questions. Traditional mass media presented audiences with information that gave them something to talk about. The agenda-setting hypothesis[1] that emerged after decades of academic study of mass media concluded that mass media do not tell people what to think, but they do provide an agenda so that people have something to think about. The Internet, on the other hand, can be used for a sharing of viewpoints and greater exchange of information among willing participants, but at the same time its authority as a source of information and the ease of scanning fragments of information can lead some people to think that it is a substitution for consulting multiple viewpoints. In this case, the information doesn't give people something to think about, but actually does tell people what to think because of the order of information and the appearance of quality; the speed of access can be thought of as a substitute for thoughtful consideration of the information. The act of browsing is very different from reading any text from start to finish; the ability to quickly click from one link to another registers impressions on the mind that are influenced by the page design as well as the number of competing pop-up ads or scrolling text that accompanies so many of the Internet sites we access.

Age, experience, and education influence the way a person accepts or rejects information at face value, but the real ability to comprehend information comes from the influence of the dominant media anyone, of any age, consumes. Matures tend to enjoy reading newspapers and magazines and are consumers of talk radio. Baby Boomers relate to the visual messages of television and the formats that television has traditionally used. Generations X, Y, and C each have a greater reliance on the Internet for news and information, but they differ as to what type of content they seek, or post themselves, to the Internet. For the youngest members of the Internet information sector, the elements of age, experience, and education may not have prepared them yet, for becoming *technologically literate* and understanding the quality of the messages they consume. As the pace of life continues to accelerate, reinforced by cell phone and Internet communication, it becomes easier for those groups to uncritically accept what is easily accessible.

Many teachers cringe when they read student research papers that rely only on Internet sources. One reason Boomer or Mature teachers feel this way is that they had the experience of browsing library shelves, taking time to evaluate and cross-check information, and think about the information before committing their research to paper. The act of thinking before writing structured their thought processes. Some older adults even talk of the sensual experience of picking up a pen and committing their thoughts to paper, where the act of writing by hand reinforced formal training in thinking and writing. Many of them still have difficulty in editing their work on a computer screen, where the display features allow you to only see a few paragraphs at a time, rather than an entire document that can be touched and manipulated. The other reason so many teachers are dismayed by research papers compiled entirely by Internet sources is that students seem not to understand the difference between blogs, corporate Web sites, and more thoughtfully conducted research sites. Even the ability to cut and paste information from the Internet can result in quotes out of context, and worse, outright plagiarism. As people use the Internet for information about health care, for example, it is important to understand whether the information accessed is a corporate statement about a certain drug or a product endorsed by an organization that would profit from a sale of that item.

When the dominant media used present information quickly, and in fragments, such as brief stories that provide links to others, the human thought processes also become more fragmented and less contextual. When students compose their research papers on computers, they often rely on grammar and spelling programs to monitor their work. The ability to compose easily, print out a paper that looks clean and well organized, or hit the "send" button before proofreading often results in funny phrases that would embarrass students, if they took the time to read what they write. One example is that of a student who was writing of the intention of the framers of the Constitution who submitted a paper crediting the "four fathers of our nation" when she meant to write the "fore-fathers of our nation."

The following topics provide a number of examples to show how using computers, the Internet, and cell phones with Internet functionality, leads to fragmentary thinking, and questions the integrity of information when it can be so easily manipulated in digital form. From posting information to manipulating the content of messages, digital information is easily corrupted, though it may still appear to be factual and professional. Our copyright laws regarding ownership of information were written when traditional print media were considered the primary media of information exchange, and content was fixed in a tangible medium. Today, digital information and the open architecture of the Internet elevate questions of validity and ownership. As a result, the ability of a person to manipulate digital data raises questions about originality, and whether those earlier laws can still be applied to today's media. The transitory nature of digital information resides in a "placeless" state, meaning that digital information can easily be erased, leading us to question whether information can be made to be permanent, or whether our culture is moving toward a future in which information itself, exists in a fragmented, transitory state. The ability to manipulate digital information visually as well as structurally leads to new attitudes and behaviors emerging in the digital era, which will undoubtedly challenge many traditional values, and contribute to new ones.

THE WIKIPEDIA PHENOMENON

Among the examples of information resources that can be collaborative, fragmented, and transitory is the online encyclopedia *Wikipedia*. The Hawaiian term *wiki* means "quick" and has been used to describe the range of programs that allow people to easily edit and share content on the Internet. While there are many different wiki platforms that can be used in office environments, in collaborative research projects, and for communication among customers and service providers in some industries, the most well known form of wiki architecture is through Wikipedia.

Anyone who uses a major search engine for general knowledge can probably attest to the growing popularity of Wikipedia as an online source of information. Since search engines present the most accessed sites in chronological order, Wikipedia sites often appear in the top group for any topic. But though Wikipedia could have what Marshall Poe calls "the potential to be the greatest effort in collaborative knowledge gathering the world has ever known,"[2] there are some problems with collaborative information gathering and storage.

Wikipedia is the brainchild of Jimmy Wales, who originally created an online community in 1999 called Nupedia.org. The idea behind Nupedia was that the content would be organized by a board of experts, and submissions would be made by people who had expertise in their own fields. Unfortunately, the site appeared the same year its biggest competitor, the *Encyclopedia Britannica*, was made available to users free, on line. Between the attention given to the free, electronic version of such a well-known collection of information and the yet untested collaborative model using a wiki platform, Nupedia did not attract the attention Wales hoped. To develop the program, Wales hired Larry Sanger, an experienced computer programmer who had a strong commitment to collaborative software and a desire to develop a system that would encourage dialogue and disagreement for stimulating discussion. On January 10, 2001, Wales and Sanger created the Nupedia wiki, but finding willing volunteer experts proved to be a problem. When Sanger developed a business model for the open source program that would allow anyone, not just a team of experts, to participate in knowledge creation and discussion and presented it to Wales, the idea of Wikipedia began to form. Sanger then launched Wikipedia as an alternative to Nupedia and created a discussion site that began to stir interest among expert and nonexpert collaborators. By the end of 2001, Wikipedia had accumulated approximately 15,000 articles.[3]

For a researcher relying on Wikipedia, the transitory nature of the information can be a problem. While anyone can post information as quickly as the push of the "send" button on a computer, information added to Wikipedia does not immediately become permanent. Wikipedians can challenge what others have written, or edit what they see. Periodically one of the volunteer editors examines the information and posts a statement regarding the question of authenticity, or removes questionable, offensive, or inaccurate information. But for the moment that something is posted, the information may appear factual and real. Within a week, information can be changed, challenged, or it can disappear. Members of the online community surrounding Wikipedia have introduced an entire new vocabulary to the collaborative venture. Those who post information are known as *Wikipedians*; when an editing decision is reversed, it is said to *revert*; *WikiGnomes* are users who quietly improve on the grammar and punctuation of the postings of others; and *WikiTrolls* are those who try to disrupt the site.

These potential pitfalls, though, don't overshadow the impact of Wikipedia as a new, collaborative venture that could become the world's largest information resource. Because the "space" Wikipedia inhabits is cyberspace, the possibility for growth is as endless as the number of topics it can include, and because of the ease of using keywords, hypertext links, and other Internet functions, Wikipedia can appear to be a pathway to greater in-depth information gathering, if the user goes beyond the initial few paragraphs for a topic. The transitory nature of a posting may be a problem, and the temporary nature of information that can change or be changed limits the utility of the information as fact, but the experiment itself is a statement on the nature of digital information and the potential for shaping the content on the Internet. Stacy Schiff writes about the content of many of the postings on Wikipedia and raises the question of how secure and factual Wikipedia information is compared with other forms of media. She writes,

> Pettiness, idiocy, and vulgarity are regular features of the site. Nothing about high-minded collaboration guarantees accuracy, and open editing invites abuse. Senators and congressmen have been caught tampering with their entries; the entire House of Representatives has been banned from Wikipedia several times. (It is not subtle to change Senator Robert Byrd's age from eighty-eight to a hundred and eighty. It is subtler to sanitize one's voting record in order to distance oneself from an unpopular President, or to delete broken campaign promises). . . . Wikipedia, which began as an experiment in unfettered democracy, has sprouted policies and procedures. At the same time the site embodies our newly casual relationship to truth.[4]

Schiff raises an important point. How do we know what we access on the Internet to be true? It could probably be said that traditional media outlets are also subject to inaccuracies, bias, and misrepresentation, but generally, over time, the assumption is that truth will emerge, especially if people consult as many sources as possible and make their own decision about the veracity of information. Is the act of submitting information to Wikipedia an assurance that the person posting the information is objective and knowledgeable? Can we be sure that information hasn't been tampered with, either innocently or by a WikiTroll? Wikipedia was designed on the principle that the collaborative nature of the project would weed out the inaccuracies, and perhaps that may happen over time, but anyone can access the information before or after any inaccuracies are caught, corrected, or deleted. The example, though, demonstrates how *open-source* media raise new questions about the quality of information and the challenges presented by collaborative models that are both transitory in time and different from models that we've learned to understand.

THE OPEN SOURCE MOVEMENT

In the world of the Internet, *open source* defines the liberating aspect of the system to be all-inclusive by allowing individuals to access free software or content and share "ownership" of material. Open source defines the original intention of the Internet before commercialization, and it is based on the idea that those who participate in Internet activities will do so in a trustworthy manner. In the case of Wikipedia, the idea that collaboration and editing serves to separate the inaccuracies from the accurate information, and that the accurate information will survive, is a part of trust in the collaborative process. But the separation of inaccuracy and accuracy takes time and is a deliberative process—which the Internet facilitates in grand form. What people tend to forget, though, is that synchronous, real-world time is necessary to allow the collaborative process to run its course. The instant access issues of using Wikipedia still need to be considered with reference to the process by which information is gathered and evaluated. Time still plays a major role in the outcome of the quality of the message.

The open source movement also deals with the aspects of freedom to use information and the nature of free software and content available on the Internet. The technical nature of digital information is that it can be easily duplicated, and the copy that is made is of equal quality to the original material. Many people who value the aspects of the Internet and digital data desire the ability to use those features without penalty, but for those people who post original information on the Internet, traditional concepts of copyright and ownership can open a Pandora's box of problems. What results is an example of how technology often precedes our ability to create rational legal structures to accommodate newer distribution forms. The open architecture of the Internet has allowed many people to think that information should be free and that they have every right to use what they want, and post whatever they like. When commercial enterprises use the Internet for profit, or when hackers or thieves violate the premise of trust just to show their technological expertise, or for profit, the integrity of everything on the Internet is called into question. The challenges afforded by these violations influence our entire basis of copyright law and our free enterprise system.

ATTITUDES TOWARD OWNERSHIP: A MATTER OF CONTROL

It isn't surprising that so many people freely download music, duplicate CDs they borrow from a library, or share video clips online. The features of the Internet and the ease of manipulating digital information easily has encouraged unauthorized access of some types of content. The Recording Industry Associa-tion of America (RIAA) has been engaged in a battle over copyright and ownership of music for years, since the original Napster program[5] made MP3 technology capable of sharing music and creating a digital music library from music played on the radio and from CD collections. It's no surprise that the technologically capa-ble younger audience became the experts on understanding, and often designing programs that could skirt around issues of copyright and licensing. The ease of duplication and the development of programs that facilitated downloading and sharing has resulted in two popular new attitudes: first, that technology liberates us from older ownership structures, and second, that if the technology exists, it must be legal to engage in these practices. No matter what avenue one pursues in thinking about these problems, all roads lead toward problems with traditional copyright legislation and the question of whether our social system will support changes to such long-held beliefs about copyright and ownership.

Copyright laws originally emerged after the invention of the printing press, when information and ideas could be made available on a fixed medium such as paper. Copyright law in the United States can be traced to the sixteenth century in Britain, where the government allowed printers to exercise copyright, and so that the government could trace seditious or damaging material to its source. The U.S. Constitution specifically includes a section in Article I, Section 8, guaranteeing authors and inventors the right of ownership to their writings and discoveries, to support the promotion of science and progress. While there have been many revisions of copyright law in the United States, the Copyright Act of 1976 clearly states that protection is given to "ownership of any original content in a fixed medium of expression." In the world of art, media, and contemporary cultural expressions of original art, copyright was the safest, most legal structure to assure that artists would be paid for their original creations and retain ownership.

Most of our media organizations, including the recording industry, television and radio broadcasters, and the film industry, were originally created with business models that featured media content owned by a company (often on behalf of an individual artist) and licensed for use by others who would pay for the privilege of using the material. In the days of digital technology, though, the entire licensing system has been jeopardized because it is so easy to download digital information freely. Young people often justify their downloading of content and naively assume that the government can and does exercise greater control over the development of new technologies. Their rationale for not paying for content is that "if it's illegal, why is it possible to do it?" Then too, they justify their own sense of morality by claiming that they are poor and wouldn't have access to the content unless it was available freely. This moral equivocation is not a sign of any inherent human weakness in character. It is part of the way humans think about justifying their actions by asserting moral superiority. In a capitalist system where free enterprise is often rewarded by new technology development and deployment, thinking of technology as an improvement, rather than a problem, is a part of our cultural belief system.

PRECEDENTS AND PROBLEMS

Copyright laws in the United States have always favored artistic expressions of content in fixed media. It is relatively easy to identify who writes a song, performs a song, and what record label produces a product, like a record or CD. When it comes to addressing the ability of *technology* to appropriate content, the laws often lack specificity. In an ideal world, our government would like to see technologies created that help audiences gain access to information and content, and our legal system is hesitant to curb the development of any technology that could be viewed as chilling (restricting) vitality in the marketplace of technological development. It is much more common, though, for a technology to be marketed first, and when that technology is found to be capable or appropriating content and skirting around matters of copyright, the courts inevitably become involved.

Some of the legal cases that serve as precedents to today's digital forms include the 1984 decision, known as the Betamax Decision, to allow people with video cassette recorders (VCRs) to record television programs for their own use; the case concerning downloading of music, known as the Grokster Decision; and the policy known as the Digital Millennium Copyright Act. Each of these legal decisions were made at specific times in history in which the role of technology as a cultural force presented a new set of situations for the courts to consider, and each has influenced every decision regarding digital information and copyright, since becoming law. While these three situations are not all-inclusive—many court battles have been fought and are currently in litigation—they do each contribute a significant legal precedent for thinking about the technologies and services that will result from a greater reliance on open source programs and technologies that facilitate traditional copyright law.

The Betamax Decision

One of the first cases to involve technology capable of recording content that was owned and controlled by others was *Sony Corp. of America, et al. v. Universal Cities Studios, Inc., et al.* (464 U.S. 417) in 1984. More commonly known as the

Betamax case, the conflict revolved around the development of the VCR and its technological capability for recording television programs directly off broadcast, for later viewing. The term "time shifting" entered our vocabulary as the Sony Corporation, maker of the Betamax VCR, and other equipment manufacturers involved in developing recording technologies touted the capability of the VCR to free viewers from the standard broadcast schedules. Not surprisingly, television content providers claimed that the VCR would violate copyright restrictions on their properties.

The original case was heard in U.S. District Court in California in 1976, and over the years, briefs were entered claiming that the VCR not only violated copyright but also introduced unfair competition into the television broadcast market. Eventually, the conflict reached the Supreme Court, where the Court's 504 ruling resulted in a statement that because the VCR could also be used for other purposes than copyright violation, such as playing prerecorded videotapes, or personally recorded home videos, the technology could, indeed, be used to time-shift for personal use. The court found that a technology could not be barred, or the makers of the technology prohibited from trade, if the technology was also capable of being used for non-copyright-infringing purposes. This landmark case opened the door for individuals to use technologies for duplicating materials for their own purposes, but the floodgates for other questions were opened. What would happen if people recorded copyrighted material and then sold the videocassettes? What if they edited material and reformatted it for their own use in another form of media? While the Betamax case gave great power to consumers, other situations were yet to emerge that contributed to a growing range of questions about user-controlled technologies, content, and ownership.

Digital Millennium Copyright Act

In 1998, the U.S. Congress passed the Digital Millennium Copyright Act to provide broad, sweeping guidelines for the development of technologies that could contribute to violating copyright law. In an area known as digital rights management (DRM), the government attempted to clarify who and what could be done in the emerging area of file sharing, copyright violations, and technology development. In short, DRM legislation attempts to protect the consumer's right to duplicate digital material for personal purposes, but penalizes companies that attempt to create technologies that induce copyright infringement with no other, more benign uses. Furthermore, DRM gives consumers control over digital information that reflects matters of personal information and personal privacy, and reaffirms the perspective that individuals have greater rights than corporations. The legislation also states that corporations cannot be restricted from competition in marketing their products.

Grokster

The second landmark case to address copyright issues and technology capable of recording copyrighted material was *Metro-Goldwin-Mayer Studios, Inc., et al., v. Grokster, Ltd., et al.* (545 U.S. 913, 2005), dealing with the emerging peer-to-peer file sharing technologies (P2P) and software that resulted in a different decision than the Betamax case. By the time this case reached the Supreme Court, a number of new technologies had flooded the market, and entertainment industries, particularly the Recording Industry Association of America (RIAA), had become more forceful about protecting their assets and their future businesses.

By 2005, when the Grokster case was heard by the Supreme Court, Grokster and Streamcast, the maker of Morpheus software that allowed individuals to freely download and share music over the Internet, had already caused the recording industry to lose millions of dollars in sales of CDs. This time, the justices felt that the Betamax Decision no longer applied as a precedent, because P2P file sharing could not be used for other purposes; instead, Grokster et al. actually *induced* copyright infringement, and therefore, was deemed illegal. The final decision, on June 27, 2006, had applicability for the music industry, which had been most severely affected to that time, but also reflected concerns of television and film industry professionals who had also feared that file sharing would result in loss of control over their media products as well. In the settlement of the case, Grokster paid $50 million to the music and recording industries, but other P2P software and technologies continued to be developed, and the growing movement to support open source programs for the Internet has continued to mount challenges to the Grokster precedent.

Though the Betamax case and the Grokster case demonstrate two different technologies that emerged at different times in history, they outline the trajectory toward increased government interest in protecting copyright in an age in which materials can so easily be digitally duplicated and freely shared. DRM is a midpoint from which the government has, and continues to find clarification in and among the many competing interests of participants in an age of digital information.

THE DIGITAL DILEMMA

When the digital aspects of material on the Internet can be manipulated, what happens to the integrity of the original material, and what personal control does an original author have to anything he or she has created? In an *Atlantic Monthly* article, James Fallows discussed the permanence of digital information.[6] His thesis was that among the various storage media such as the stone tablet, the audio cassette, the floppy disc, and the digital disc, the most reliable form of storage of information is the stone tablet. Not only can digital data stored on any other form be destroyed easily, but the technology used to access data on a tape or disc has been upgraded by new technology so often that people have entire repositories of information that they can no longer access. He writes,

> The book I wrote twenty-five years ago using that computer still looks fine—but the interview notes for it, which I "saved" on those big old disks, I might just as well have burned. For all practical purposes, there is no way for me to get at them anymore—nor at other information that over the years I've lodged on 5.25-inch disks, small archival high-density tapes, some varieties of Zip drives, and other media that my current computers can't handle. . . . A few years ago, virtually any new PC had a built-in 3.5-inch disk drive. Now such drives are often missing or optional, as CD-ROMS and DVDs have become standard . . . Any file stored more than six or eight years ago, and not transferred to something more modern in the meantime, is on its way to doom.[7]

Fallows correctly identifies some of the issues of control of digital data, both in its fixed form, and according to the nature of technological development, but again, the issues of the control of digital information are a double-edged sword. An alternate interpretation of the permanence of digital information is offered by Simson Garfinkle, who writes on the ability of people to scan information into a computer and store things digitally in ways that not only take less physical space, but also, can be easily shared electronically.[8] But Fallows and Garfinkle argue about the integrity of the format on which digital information is stored. Fallows maintains that it takes effort and expense to upgrade digital data, while Garfinkle claims that two contemporary file formats appear to have the staying power that will keep them operable no matter what, for some time to come. He claims that portable document formats (PDFs) and Joint Photographic Experts Group (JPEG) image formats have become so widely used that they are likely to exist for some time. But still, what each of these authors addresses is that *what* you save electronically is as important as the ability to save it.

Digital files of pictures and paperwork may be fine for personal records, and they can help eliminate bulky stacks of paper, but at the same time, they can be stolen or corrupted by people or programs that access someone's hard drive. When organizations collect data about you, post information about you that you are not aware of without your permission (like including your personal information in a database), you aren't even aware of the violation of your personal information until it becomes apparent—usually in a surprising way, such as finding that you're a victim of identify theft, or that your personal information can be accessed through an Internet browser. When people willingly post information on sites like MySpace, they have no knowledge of who or how many people read that information and make judgments about the person. Believing in open source models accompanies a certain abandonment of privacy and personal information and an attitude that could challenge traditional interpretations of privacy law. If there were strict guidelines and clear-cut laws, there would be greater clarity of what constitutes a violation of ownership, but in the emerging world of digital information, it's hard to adapt laws that were written for different forms of media.

Cell phones are also technologies that have the capacity to violate personal information. Certainly, a phone that records audio information without others knowing it is one type of violation. Cell phones that access the Internet face the same problems as using computers to access the Internet. The biggest problem with cell phones is the camera feature that can unobtrusively snap pictures of people in areas where privacy is assumed. It's very difficult to know when someone is unobtrusively taking your picture, but it's even more of a shock when you find that a picture of yours has been posted to the Internet or shared with others without your knowledge. Health clubs have had to enforce guidelines about not using cell phones in dressing rooms to protect the privacy of clients. Courtrooms generally prohibit the use of cell phones, so that pictures or audio can't potentially violate the privacy of the deliberations therein.

The ability to take pictures without other people knowing they are being photographed reflects both privacy issues and the right of a person to his or her own image. It may be true that bystanders have occasionally used cell phone pictures to photograph a crime or identify a criminal,[9] or that cell phone pictures can document events that can be posted to the Internet for all to see (like the execution of Saddam Hussein), but for the most part, these extreme examples show how difficult it is to separate the positive aspects of technological features from the negative ones that can be used to violate privacy, too.

Legal Loopholes and Emerging Markets

Most attempts at legislation concerning ownership of information so far have separated issues of violations of copyright for forms of media, like music, film, or television, from commercial harvesting of information for profit, and personal use of digital material for self-expression. In this negotiation, big media industries fear losing control over their properties, commercial marketers or information harvesters view the information accessible over the Internet as free data, and individuals feel that anything on the Internet should be available to them for use. The result has left all of the traditional media industries scrambling for new markets, hoping to gain a foothold in areas that currently are subject to newly negotiated rules, regulations, and laws.

Some of the organizations most concerned with control over ownership of media content, are the legacy companies that base their entire business models and economic structures around the ability to sell and make a profit on media content. Traditional media companies are well aware of consumer habits and the changing patterns of American time that attracts consumers with shorter attention spans and the ability to comprehend information in briefer, more fragmented ways. The recording industry was the first to experience the threat of losing control over its business as MP3 technologies made sharing audio files so easy for consumers. Visual content takes more bandwidth to transfer and though more people are continually upgrading their technology with computers that have better space management hardware, broadband delivery to the home, and clearer visual displays on monitors, television and film content isn't far behind. Already, the television and film industries have tried to anticipate the shift from traditional television, VCR, DVD, and film distribution forms to direct delivery of content over the Internet.

Some of their efforts so far have resulted in the growing DVD market for episodic television series, and a cultivation of the potential cell phone market, which would rely on effectively communicating over a small screen. The aesthetics of these shifts balance consumer behavior and audience demographics that reflect who might be interested in using smaller, portable technologies for news, information, and entertainment. Television producers know that many people have busy lifestyles and may not be able to watch a favorite television show, or even record it for later viewing. This has resulted in episodic television series that consumers might access in an On Demand feature, or by renting or purchasing a series' collected episodes on DVD. If and when these programs are available over the Internet, questions of unauthorized duplication or payment structures would also have to be clarified. If they aren't, the revenue from advertising—the lifeblood of the television industry—could be undermined.

While the potential cell phone market is still in its infancy, legacy companies have been experimenting with content and delivery to see if there is a real market for television delivery over cell phones or the Internet. Every media content provider has been forced to consider the impact of the Internet on their business. The Consumer Electronics Show in 2006 was inundated with examples of what cell phone and Internet providers hope will be the future of content delivery. Cell phone providers have been particularly interested in entering the news and entertainment content business because there are so few rules and regulations as yet, for how this type of business can create revenue, and the service can be paid for by subscription. Verizon has developed V Cast, a high speed cellular network that delivers Internet-quality video over broadband in wireless form, to subscribers who can choose from over 300 video clips, most of which are two to three minutes long. V Cast uses content from CNN, sports briefs from ESPN, and a number of Comedy Central programs like *The Daily Show with Jon Stewart*. They view the market as the younger segment of the population who tend to upgrade their cell phones regularly and who are among the most "mobile" members of society. Cingular and Sprint also offer subscription video services through MobiTV, which provides over twenty channels of television programming from mainstream sources, including NBC News, Fox Sports, and C-Span.[10] Senior vice president of News Corporation, Lucy Hood, describes the emerging cell phone market as an opportunity for traditional telecom companies to become involved in the lucrative content delivery market in this way: "You always have your phone with you. If you can pick up your phone and see one minute or five minutes of media that you enjoyed, that's a rich media experience in its own way. So that's what we're creating for."[11]

Commercial Manipulation

Although legacy media companies have ownership rights to creative content, and are working to establish new markets in different forms of delivery, different legal issues are involved when commercial enterprises trade in digital data that potentially violates personal privacy. The Digital Millennium Copyright Act specifies that every commercial service should have an "opt out" section on its Internet sites, but policing the number of sites that are often operated anonymously, or are hidden by the architecture of the Internet, is much harder to determine. The result is a number of local and regional efforts to create state laws that further define privacy. Zizi Papacharissi and Jan Fernback conducted a study of the online privacy statements available on several sites and concluded that these statements seldom provided reassurances that are intended to be upheld by the DRM. They conclude that these statements generally are written to protect the companies sponsoring the site, rather than protecting the privacy of the individuals who use them.[12]

Personal Use

What characterizes Generation C is an ease of manipulating digital information and thinking of digital content as material in the public domain. Generation C, in particular, and Generation Y, to some degree, have become masters of taking digital information from other forms and modifying it for their own purposes. *Mashups* are combinations of mixed media that take content from other forms and are put together in a new way. Examples are disc jockeys who mix sounds take copyrighted material and manipulate it for their own presentations, and individuals who are capable of putting parody or satirical videos together for posting on MySpace, Flickr, or their own blogs, but do these personal manipulations of content violate copyright? Are the new forms copyrightable in their own form? These issues have yet to be debated in courts, but we can reasonably assume a test case will be in the near future. In the meantime, the effect of these activities shows how the combination of forces, including material formerly controlled by institutions that held copyrights and licenses, and technologies that give access to individuals to duplicate, manipulate, and repost, all contribute to a culture in which some of the traditional expectations are being challenged by new practices.

THE PERSONAL AND THE PRIVATE

What happens in the world of the Internet is a blurring of what is commercial and what is personal. The heart of the problem is the issue that commercial ventures can masquerade as private postings on the Internet. Barb Palser writes that in May 2006, a two-minute video clip on MySpace, titled "Al Gore's Penguin Army," was submitted by a person who identified himself or herself as "toutsmith." His MySpace profile identified him as a 29-year-old male from Beverly Hills, California. The clip spoofed Gore's documentary, *An Inconvenient Truth*, about the problem of global warming, and within three months, the clip had registered nearly 60,000 hits. On August 3, the *Wall Street Journal* exposed the clip as the handiwork of the DCI Group, a Republican public relations firm.[13]

It's difficult to say with accuracy who owns material that is posted on the Internet and who takes responsibility for verifying the accuracy of the information. The Internet is open to postings that reflect different opinions and interpretations, and various tools and levels of skill allow any amateur the ability to post information that looks as credible and factual as that posted by media institutions that have been assumed to have compiled their information fairly, and ethically (though this statement alone could open up an entirely new avenue of discussion).

Issues reflecting the quality and veracity of information and the control of that information all suggest a platform on which future laws will be tested and evaluated. Personal habits toward browsing information that is so readily available and an ability to think critically about the quality and source material of the content is imperative for democratic underpinnings of using information that is stored and made accessible on the Internet.

As people begin to look for faster ways to accomplish tasks, the time they are willing to devote to looking for information and the time elements of the technology structure expectations for quick results. Young people are particularly vulnerable to such activity, since the dominant media they use are digital, and present information in quick, but fragmented way; if someone clicks from link to link, and accepts what they see or read as truthful, they may not realize how often the information they have accessed reflects the attitudes, biases, and sometimes, unethical purposes of the person or business that posted it. Even if they start with a solid authority, the links and clicks they make can lead to accessing opinions and assertions, rather than facts.

The Internet is continually being bombarded by companies that hope to use the medium as a way to generate profit. From Google maps that use satellites to show images of faraway places to services that allow advertising on Web pages, Internet users are bombarded by fast-moving visual and audio stimulus that reacts with the person's senses to lay a series of impressions on the person's mind. Most of these impressions are formed quickly, and because the technologies used are so personal, the effects are remarkable.

The ease of using these messages and the growing market for using the Internet for both commercial as well as unethical purposes have raised a number of legal questions that incorporate matters of information ownership and privacy. What is perhaps most challenging, though, is the tenuous relationship this proposes between individuals and government. Should the government take active steps to protect citizens who uncritically use technologies and services that result in any number of social problems? How can the rights of one person be protected, when other people could also be affected by any laws restricting their own use of these technologies? The answers to all of these questions raise important discussions that reflect a number of competing viewpoints. Among all of the issues is whether the Internet will continue to function as it does, or whether major changes will be in the offing.

WILL THE INTERNET REMAIN FREE?

The nature of information is at the heart of issues surrounding digital data, and the Internet as a storehouse of personal and commercial material. The way people use this information can be creative and liberating and can result in stronger relationships that underscore democratic principles and values. At the same time, though, there is evidence that the proliferation of technologies and services that give people the potential to access and share information may be resulting in less knowledge, rather than more. N. Abramovitz and Guilio A. De Leo write that so far, more information has not resulted in a population that is better informed. Instead, it has probably contributed to more information with less critical thought.[14] Citing a number of studies about what citizens know about politics and history, Abramovitz and De Leo claim that in the last thirty years, knowledge of popular culture has grown, but matters of civic importance have declined. The authors blame the growing lack of interest in significant matters on the number of media forms that digest information and sanitize it in the simplest way, abstracting meaning from the context and interpreting meaning through abstracted material.

David Talbot writes about how the Internet has become inundated with so much information that is fluff, meaningless, and sometimes dangerous, saying that it is now time for a "clean-slate" approach toward revising and reinventing the Internet.[15] He writes,

> Indeed, for the average user, the Internet these days all too often resembles New York's Times Square in the 1980s. It was exciting and vibrant, but you made sure to keep your head down, lest you be offered drugs, robbed, or harangued by the insane. Times Square has been cleaned up, but the Internet keeps getting worse, both at the user's level, and . . . deep within its architecture. . . . For all of the Internet's wonders, it is also difficult to manage and more fragile with each passing day.[16]

Have the problems of information and data storage become so great that our futures will undergo even greater change? The final chapters investigate what social technologies and practices have already receded in American life and how our culture is likely to adopt the new principles afforded by the shift to digital information, and the convenience of cell phones and the Internet.

Eight

Where Have All the Phone Booths Gone?

When technologies work well, we experience a rush of control and satisfaction with our decisions to use them; but when they fail us, we can sometimes feel frustrated, annoyed, and helpless. One day you might forget your cell phone and have to search for a pay phone, only to notice that there are none to be found in the old, familiar places. You might receive an e-card for your birthday from a friend and feel that something very personal is missing. Is there anything more annoying that calling a public company, only to be shifted from one recording device to another, with no option to talk to a human customer service operator? However subtle the change, every person, sometimes, realizes that things aren't what they used to be.

The process of subtle, incremental cultural change is a difficult phenomenon for most people to comprehend. Most people are too busy to stop and think about how little changes affect our daily lives unless something goes wrong, and technology can be blamed for upsetting the daily balance. Some of the shifts in American culture that have been most affected by cell phones and the Internet have to do with a loss of public conveniences and public institutions that we once thought were staples of American life. The shift we are experiencing is part of the technologically induced movement away from public technologies and institutions designed for the mass audience and toward the more individually centered, private use of technology and media content. Some of these changes are observable; public conveniences, like public telephones, are harder to find, and trying to speak to a customer service representative when calling any company or government organization is almost impossible, since prerecorded messages prompt us to push buttons to access preprogrammed answers to a range of questions. Communities, which were once only geographically bound, now also exist in cyberspace. The institutions we counted on to protect our liberties and freedoms, like government and law enforcement institutions, are struggling to adapt to electronic information processes that cast our previous democratic practices and legal protections into question. Most of all, the proliferation of technologies that serve an individual's need and desire for communication, information, and connection to society have disrupted traditional social expectations and practices. The following sections examine what we've lost and what we've gained in contemporary society, as personal technologies have shifted traditional relationships between public and private activities.

MATTERS OF CONVENIENCE: CHANGING BUSINESS MODELS AND CULTURAL INSTITUTIONS

There is no doubt that using a cell phone is much more convenient than searching for a public phone, finding a battered phone booth, and scrambling to come up with the right change to make a call, but when a cell phone fails you because you can't get service or the battery has gone dead, using the battered phone booth looks a much better option than not being able to make a call at all. Since cell phones became popular, the numbers of public telephones have decreased, and in some places these telephones have been removed altogether. Not long ago, public telephones were a main source of the telephone industry's profits. Airports are one of the few remaining public places where a person can find pay phones, but even there, their number has diminished, and the cost of making a call on a public phone has skyrocketed. Ashley Simonsen writes of the decrease in the number of pay phones at Logan Airport in Boston, from 771 to 550 between 1999 and 2003.[1] During the same four-year period, the cost of making a call rose from 25 cents to 50 cents for a local call and long-distance charges changed from rates tied to distance and time on line, to a flat $4 a minute. These changes directly reflect the growth of the cell phone market and the lower-cost pricing structures that cell phone providers began to offer over the same period.

Eventually we will probably use public wireless services to make calls with the aid of our personal cell phones. Many telecom companies have plans to offer wireless VoIP technology to aid those who don't have a cell phone (or those who forgot to charge their batteries), but these systems are not yet widely used. VoIP has already begun to offer home and business subscribers lower-cost phone service over the Internet, and as already demonstrated, the private uses of VoIP have resulted in better service, lower costs, and greater consumer satisfaction with the quality of the call, but companies in the United States have not yet dealt with the complexity of developing wireless systems in public places capable of handling the necessary amount of telephone and data traffic.

Once wireless VoIP technologies are publicly available, cell phones may be used as personal tools to connect to the Internet, much as laptop computers are. For the computer literate, this will probably be an easy transition, but for the older population that doesn't carry laptops, or for whom using cell phones has not become second nature, another digital divide could emerge that marginalizes older generations or those who can't afford their own personal multifunction phones. The gulf between technological innovation and mass distribution of reliable systems may close over time, but the need for services is continuous and will inevitably result in disappointment and frustration for those caught in the middle. Younger users will probably be among the most willing to upgrade their current cell phones and computers to take advantage of the wireless systems and the most likely to take the lead in adopting new services. As the infrastructure for using cell phones and the Internet migrates to a more wireless platform, other institutions on which we've relied are also examining how they may be forced to change with respect to cell phones and the Internet as they become a larger part of many people's daily lives.

LEGACY COMPANIES: NEW BUSINESS MODELS AND STRATEGIES

Obviously, the companies leading the movement toward greater use of digital technology are the telecommunications firms that rely on cell phones and the Internet for their businesses, but other institutions are also adapting to new distribution forms for their content. Traditional media companies are scrambling to participate in the digital revolution on a number of fronts and are attempting to deal with the problem of shifting media content to more individually oriented, on-demand delivery formats, with new business models to maintain their revenues. Instead of developing media content for a *mass* audience, they need to consider how to facilitate direct delivery to private individuals.

As mentioned in Chapter 7, one motivation for legacy media companies to become involved in cell phone and Internet distribution is to capitalize on the inadequacies of traditional regulatory and legal structures to monitor their activities, but another reason for their interest in cultivating an audience for cell phone and Internet content is their belief that younger consumers—those who are among the major cell phone users and Internet aficionados—are the most desirable audience for advertising and maintaining their revenue streams. Most of the traditional media companies were not in the vanguard of seeking new distribution opportunities, but instead were forced to consider changing their business models only after their audience numbers began to decline.

The television industry has had to deal with the problem of delivering content to different types of visual display units, from the two-inch cell phone screen to the computer monitor, but has also had to deal with the problem of consumers using technologies that eliminate commercials. By the end of 2006, 97 percent of the digital cable subscribers in the United States had video on demand (VOD) services that allow viewers to choose what they watch and when to watch it. Many cable companies have underwritten the cost of offering VOD services or have made them available to subscribers at a low cost, but in return have specific data telling them how many viewers choose to watch specific programs available on VOD. Additional technologies like digital video recorders (DVRs) or commercial services like TiVo allow audiences to fast-forward through commercials or skip advertising altogether.[2]

The most significant change in the distribution of televised content over the Internet is in the way individuals watch television—alone and on their personal, intimate forms of media. According to a 2006 survey of 10,000 households with Internet connections, one out of every 10 households reported that someone in the home watched television shows over the Internet.[3] Most often, the Internet television consumer watched news, but approximately one-half also watched entertainment programs, with *Desperate Housewives*, *CSI*, and *The Office* being the most popular ones accessed over the Internet that year. More importantly, these programs were likely to be viewed by a single person watching alone, who downloaded the program from the Internet to the computer or to a portable device like a PDA or an iPod. In 2002, the *Economist* featured an in-depth survey of the future of television: "Many observers believe that as this trend continues, and audiences splinter into ever-smaller pieces, the social experience of TV will fragment too. This will spell the end of an era when watching TV together (in time if not in space) has provided whole countries with some sort of cultural glue, and the beginning of something more individualistic."[4]

The television industry has also had to consider how these new distribution forms call for a different visual aesthetic than required for traditional television viewing. Primary colors such as yellow, rather than gold, or blue, instead of aqua, and graphics that are simple, with easy-to-read fonts, transfer to small screens well and can be seen more clearly in a variety of environments from bright sunlight to dark locations with artificial light.[5] Small screens also don't register images that have a lot of movement, and television programs are now shot with a different "look" so that they can be adapted to different presentational forms.

The film industry has had a long history of trying to protect its business as other technologies become available. Television posed the first major threat in the late 1940s and early 1950s by bringing consumers information and entertainment in their homes rather than in public movie theaters. When the VCR was developed in the 1970s, Jack Valenti, the president of the Motion Picture Association of America, proclaimed that it was as threatening to the movies as the Boston Strangler was to a woman walking alone.[6] Although film executives may have worried that videocassettes, and later DVDs, would inevitably damage their industry, they capitalized on distributing their films to the home market. By 2006, video rentals accounted for 46 percent of the studio revenues, while box office receipts at theaters accounted for only 24 percent.[7] Hollywood also responded to the different age groups that reflected the home and theatrical release markets, and it began creating movies that would appeal the most to the teenage groups—who still frequented movie theaters while other age groups migrated to home entertainment services.

Hollywood also effectively capitalized on creating special effects films that audiences would want to see on large theater screens, and on computer-generated graphics and animation that have resulted in significantly lower production costs for both special effects films and animated features. Today, computer-generated images make up the bulk of Hollywood's animated entertainment content, but Hollywood no longer is the special place for movie magic that it once was. Matt Brady writes, "Fifty years ago, there were about 1,000 animators in Hollywood— half of them at Disney. Today, there are countless digital animators, effects specialists, and videogame makers in every major city. . . . From the wackiest cartoon to the grittiest docudrama, the true golden age of animation has just begun."[8]

Many have speculated that the growth of low-cost consumer grade video cameras and in-home computer editing systems have resulted in a growing number of independent films created by amateur filmmakers or videographers. For most of these individuals, MySpace and Flickr are tremendous distribution venues. The growth of consumer-made shorts, features, and documentaries, all available on the Internet, show that private citizens can be creative and make their work available to the public, but the traditional film industry has had to protect its future by cultivating new audiences for even more outrageous cinematic content, to keep people buying tickets, or renting content. Like the television industry, the film industry is also concerned about matters of copyright and ownership, and it, too, is scrambling to maintain its business in a time of digital distribution.

Perhaps the legacy industry that has suffered the most from the growth of Internet news, blogging, and general information is the newspaper industry. Newspaper readership has been in decline since the 1940s, but nothing has affected the newspaper industry like the immediacy of the Internet as a source of news and information. To try to counter the trend, newspapers have begun to cater to younger audiences and have attempted to improve their own online readership, but surprisingly, the greatest consumers of online news are Boomers and Matures, especially those with incomes between $100,000 and $150,000. The Audit Bureau of Circulations, an industry division that tracks readership, reported that traditional paid circulation of newspapers in the United States declined 2.6 percent in 2005, but Neilsen's NetRatings division, which monitors growth in Internet hits, shows that in the same period, online access to newspapers rose by 11 percent.[9] There is no doubt that newspaper publishers are concerned about the drop in traditional newspaper circulation and see the growth in the online business as a sign for hope, if they can continue to capture readers.

Many surveys have been conducted to find out what newspaper readers like, and overwhelmingly, their responses tend to cluster around the desire for local news and information. Additionally, respondents to a comprehensive survey about the role of newspapers in American life reported that they like newspapers that are readable and have several features rather than straight news stories.[10] If newspaper publishers continue to refashion newspapers to appeal to consumers who also use Internet services or cell phone news services, they, too, will have to examine how the traditional newspaper will function in a society where electronic information sources deliver news faster, more conveniently, and more directly to consumers.

What all legacy industries above have in common is that their traditional businesses are undergoing changes. The Internet is one of the driving forces behind those changes, and each industry has made attempts or plans to deal with revising their practices and business models to remain competitive. Although industry executives claim that they are optimistic for new avenues of revenue, most, if they are being honest, admit that their greatest fears probably have to do with losing control over their content and losing their traditional sources of revenue.

All three of these industries have traditionally relied on advertising and direct sales or rentals of their properties for their revenue. In an online world, though, there is no direct sale of media content. Sure, many people pay service providers for access to the Internet, but how can content be created to attract people to buy things? How is the advertising industry remaking itself to accommodate online delivery of traditional media content?

TOWARD A POINT-AND-CLICK CULTURE

Digital technologies that allow consumers to control traditional television delivery to the home, such as VCRs, digital video recorders (DVRs), and devices like TiVo, all threaten the traditional television advertising business, since audiences can fast-forward, delete, or even skip commercials altogether. Newspaper advertising, which has traditionally underwritten the cost of producing newspapers, is a substantial source of revenue for the newspaper industry and offsets the purchase price of a newspaper. Product placement, often referred to by media industries as *product enhancement,* has become a mainstay of underwriting production costs for both television and film.

Since the emergence of competition for consumer attention, advertising industry practices have evolved into an elaborate quest for identifying how to quantify advertising effectiveness, deliver audiences to clients, and motivate consumers to buy products. The Internet has provided a potentially lucrative alternative to traditional advertising because the results are so easily monitored. Advertisers can immediately know how many Internet users click on ads, what links they follow, and whether they buy or not. The marketing consultant Richard Yanowitch says, "The Internet is the most ubiquitous experimental lab in history, built on two-way, real-time interactions with millions of consumers whose individual consumption patterns can for the first time be infinitesimally measured, monitored, and molded."[11] What Yanowitch refers to are the many tools, such as cookies, registrations, and subscription techniques, which provide Internet advertisers with specific information about Internet users.

Search engines such as Google, Yahoo!, and MSN all sell advertising, and even user-based sites such as MySpace and Facebook are supported by advertising revenue. Seeing how lucrative the online advertising business can be, America On Line (AOL) paid $25 million for Weblogs, Inc., a conglomeration of advertising blogs that range from consumer survey reports to advice columns. The traditional television, film, and newspapers that have already become available for Internet delivery are already accompanied by a range of ads from pop-ups and pop-unders to embedded links to advertising sites. This type of efficiency for the advertising industry is a serious threat to traditional media forms, and the transition period from the old business models to the new are rife with subtle but important changes.

Although these legacy companies are all searching for new business models to insure their businesses survive, and can project growth, these subtle changes lead one to speculate on whether the Internet may eventually become more like the traditional media industries. As discussed, the features of the Internet and cell phones, which are also subject to downloading content from the Internet, are used as personal media, so as the industries seek individual consumers rather than mass audiences, what becomes of the traditional social arrangements that have guided and underscored social behavior? Will we become a society of individual consumers who compulsively point, click, and buy on a whim? Furthermore, will we be able to consume anytime, anywhere?

INTERACTING OR REACTING IN PUBLIC PLACES

Other chapters in this book have dealt with the issue of cyberspace as a community that is not grounded in a geographic space. Internet communities result from individuals' needs to go beyond the physical world to take advantage of interacting with others in a placeless environment where they don't have the trappings of their own physical bodies.

Cyberspace communities can be wonderful ways to go beyond the limits of physical space, and they have no boundaries; a cyberspace community can be truly global, and interactions can be multicultural, diverse, and exciting for their novelty and freedom. At the same time, participation in cyberspace communities are often short lived, fulfilling personal needs until the desire to participate in the community changes, or the cyberspace community is no longer maintained by participants.

Public Places and Personal Needs

What also happens, though, in the cyber community is that all interaction is vicarious, and though some aspects of interaction can be rewarding, *most* people still need to feel the energy of human interaction, too. The growth of telecommuting (working from home or private space instead of in a traditional office) has reinforced the notion that people still seem to need some social environment to feel the balance in their lives. The growth in Internet cafés, where individuals can bring laptops and take advantage of high-speed wireless connections, has also resulted in an intriguing social phenomenon. While Internet cafés were originally designed to allow people to sit quietly for a while, use their laptops, and drink coffee or have a snack, they have often been used by telecommuters, or people who need wireless connections to the Internet, as substitute offices.

An article in the *Boston Sunday Globe* identified some of the problems that Internet café owners are now experiencing. Alison Lobron writes, "Some wireless users sneak in their own food with their laptops. Others buy one cup of coffee at 9 a.m. and surf the Net until closing time. And the truly audacious sit for hours without making any pretense of a purchase."[12] The article explains that Internet café owners face a dilemma of how to limit seating availability for those who don't purchase anything, but tie up café space, and of whether or not to offer free wireless services, but the message is much more important. People are social animals and occasionally need the stimulation of other people. In this case, private interactions are moving to public places, to fulfill the human need to be around others.

Other places where people have traditionally gone for social purposes are also changing. One of the areas that have attracted a considerable amount of attention is the way online shopping has changed the experience of shopping in a store and the resulting impact on consumer behavior in private versus public places.

Shopping has traditionally been a public activity.[13] As previously discussed, the most likely candidates to embrace online shopping are those for whom using the Internet is familiar and comfortable. Retailers have long been interested in exploring potential new markets and have found the Internet an efficient avenue to reach consumers. The result is that many brick-and-mortar stores now have smaller showrooms and larger Internet databases of stock. When goods can be ordered either online or in a store, and shipped to consumers through a mail service, the cost of display space, the number of employees, and the costs of doing retail business are reduced. What is also reduced is the shopper's ability to see or touch the product. Reliance on the visual image online is an important feature of online shopping, but it changes the social experience of the store as a social space and the tactile experience of touching a product or item.

Time in history is the element at play in the growth of online shopping. While retailers have tempted consumers with enhancements to use the Internet for shopping by promising convenience, easy return plans, and other incentives for purchasing online, most consumers were wary of Internet shopping because of the threat of credit card fraud or misleading ads. The online retailing business first became profitable in 2001, but many people worried that payment information could easily be hacked or robbed, and many sites were difficult to maneuver. By the holiday season in 2003, enough privacy protection had been promised or assured, and enough trust developed in using the Internet, to register record numbers of sales in online purchases. By 2005, several companies reported that online retailing had surpassed in-store sales. Timberland Co., a popular catalog retailer, registered an increase of 137 percent in online holiday sales on Cyber Monday, 2005, the name given to the Monday after Thanksgiving, as the Christmas shopping season began.[14]

Many traditional brick-and-mortar stores have tried to create environments that help customers feel comfortable. They realize that the Internet can threaten their businesses, and they know that to increase foot traffic, they have to redesign their environments to attract people to come in and spend time in the stores. Barnes and Noble has mastered the art of presenting a comfortable environment for people to shop, but has also limited the amount of seating so that too many people don't stay too long. The environment promises comfort and leisure, but still encourages browsing and purchasing.

No doubt, Internet shopping is convenient and may also allow a consumer the opportunity of comparing products and prices online, but Internet shoppers are also subject to new business models that encourage spending. The genius behind Amazon's retailing efforts, Jeff Bezos, developed a system of online retailing that not only alerts potential customers when a new book or product comes onto the market, but also tracks the customers' purchasing records to increase the direct marketing of new products. This effective use of the computer and the Internet's ability to send information two ways has the same potential to abuse personal information, but has been so skillfully developed in the Amazon model, that the personal, intimate communication characteristics of the technology outweigh the question of the storage of personal information and the potential for data mining.

BUSINESS PRACTICES AND SOCIAL VALUES

The way people think about their surroundings, the activities in which they engage, and the way they interact with others is the result of a combination of forces that are both unique and structured by social contexts and the technologies we use. As the institutions we rely on to help us sustain our daily lives change, through adaptation to new technologies, and accommodate the new behaviors that those technologies elicit, we find that our culture is most certainly changing.

The technologies that define a generation are critical arbiters of cultural change, and for those who deal with multigenerational groups of people, there are good reasons to try to understand what motivates people of different age groups. John C. Beck and Mitchell Wade present an alarming, but intriguing, picture of how gaming techniques have influenced the younger segment of today's workforce. They claim that today's worker who might be in their twenties or thirties (Generations C, Y, and X) are individuals who have "never known a time without digital games,"[15] and that as a result, they've developed a unique set of values that they bring to the workplace. Among the attitudes gamers bring to business is a sense that they themselves see their roles in an organization as special individuals whose attributes are more important than the overall goals of the organization. They approach problems with an attitude of trying different things and a belief in trial and error, and they demonstrate an attitude of superiority based on their age (and the flexible thinking they believe they bring) and a belief in competition. The gamers grew up in an age overpowered by Baby Boomer attitudes and values and see themselves as a smaller group that is entitled to success.[16] Generation gaps have always reflected cohort beliefs and attitudes that are structured by the social conditions that surrounded their own coming of age, and as younger employees enter the workforce, we can see how their familiarity with instant communication technologies enhance attitudes of control. As these gamers approach jobs in some of the legacy industries that are also undergoing change, and as social institutions that mediate the sense of human connections also change, we gain a distinct vantage point from which to evaluate the potential for cultural change in the future.

THE QUIET ACQUIESCENCE TO CULTURAL CHANGE

The examples in this chapter reflect how American culture has responded to the growth of digital technologies such as cell phones and the Internet. The brief examples of how traditional media industries and some of the most basic activities in which we engage, such as shopping, show how institutions are attempting to deal with the competition the Internet poses for traditional activities. The businesses discussed so far are only examples of social institutions that are undergoing change, but the most important social group for the effective socialization of an individual still remains the family unit.

Questions concerning family interaction have also been a concern for those who observe family members spending less time together and more time consuming their own personal media. Echoing the early days of television, when the demise of the family unit was predicted as people stopped talking and began passively watching television, use of personal media can disrupt family communication patterns or at least change the nature of those interactions. For the parent and child who text each other with short messages, keeping in touch may be easier, but the quality of the interaction may also be more fragmented and less meaningful. Many scholars question whether these actions are leading us toward behaviors that substitute reacting to people, rather than communicating with them.

The patterns we adopt while using technologies such as cell phones and the Internet have enormous consequences for how we interact with other people. We generally become socialized with others through interaction. Children learn from watching adults as role models and mimicking behaviors. Few of us can actually remember why we developed attitudes that are similar to our parents, but we all remember the first time our own personal value system clashed with our parents' expectations, and what an upsetting emotional response we had to the clash of values.

As we change our own personal communication patterns to accommodate new technology, we internalize the same types of controls the technologies exert over us. We think faster, often more superficially, and in a more fragmented way. Our conversation is peppered with speech that reflects the shorter interactions of cell phone calls or instant-messaging jargon. Digital thinking replaces the type of linear thought that reading print, such as books, magazines, and newspapers, present us, and we tend to skim materials and accept information that is more prominently featured by color or type rather than reading sequentially or considering facts.

Our capacity for self-expression is also a result of whether we maintain personal face-to-face relationships or whether we substitute mediated interactions for personal connections. Getting an electronic sympathy card doesn't match the sentiment of a hug or a smile, or a handwritten personal message from someone we know, who took time to choose the card and thought about the sentiment they wrote.

THE PATH TO NEW VALUES

As the chapters in this book attest, cell phones and the Internet are contributing to new behaviors, attitudes, and cultural values. Traditional institutions are changing to exploit the features of digital communication technologies, and the young are leading the way toward a world that embraces instant communication, that may be fragmented and transitory. Time and place are no longer constrained by synchronicity or geographic boundaries.

Many of the cultural changes are subtle, and our preoccupation with getting through the busy day often prevents our noticing the process of change—what we gain and what we lose. Sadly, we may miss the realization that digital technologies are actually contributing to the speedup of daily life, and like a hamster, we find ourselves caught on the wheel—running faster and faster, but getting nowhere. If we were to stop and question the impact of technologies such as cell phones and the Internet, would we continue to use them? Or, can we be content to believe that they provide us with control, or an illusion of control, so that we chose to minimize their impact so as not to be overcome by them?

As we get caught up in the speed of life, our expectations for what life could or should be are subject to a wide range of factors that influence our social balance and the way we think of ourselves in relation to others and in relation to our society. As we participate in a world that is also experiencing a range of cultural shifts as digital technology enters traditional domains, we, as Americans, need to view our own culture with respect to the way other cultures are also changing. In the final chapter, the role of American culture in a global society underscores how cell phones and the Internet play a pivotal role in reconstructing issues of time and space, public and private activities, and changing values beyond our own borders.

Nine

Living in the Global Village

The best predictions about how cell phones and the Internet will continue to contribute to changes in how we live, work, and play are subject to multiple scenarios that reflect domestic and international events. These same technologies are contributing to cultural changes in countries around the world in a number of ways. The Internet is already a global phenomenon, and cell phones are becoming more available in both rich and poor countries. In many areas that lacked a wired telephone infrastructure, cell phones and wireless communications, either over the Internet or within regional wireless areas, have already surpassed the use and the quality of cell phone technology in the United States. In this concluding chapter, the impact of cell phones and the Internet in American life is juxtaposed against a changing global picture of cultural change, and the question to explore is whether these technologies are contributing to a world that is becoming a global village.

The innovations and institutions that existed before cell phones and the Internet have influenced the American experience. As demonstrated, audience acceptance of new technologies and services is always subject to the interplay of social, technological, and cultural forces specific to a particular time in history. If Hurricane Katrina hadn't devastated an entire region in the south of the United States, it is unlikely that the U.S. government would have looked so favorably on empowering telecommunications industries to implement a large-scale regional wireless delivery system; if the information and images of military actions in Iraq were not closely guarded by policies of the Bush administration, perhaps bloggers from around the world wouldn't be so avidly engaging in critiques of U.S. foreign policy on the Internet; if the Internet had been able to develop without hackers and profiteers, we might have been able to address laws and regulations for peer-to-peer file sharing sooner, and in a more equitable manner; if our social environments were healthy, fulfilling, and available to everyone, perhaps fewer people would be reaching out to others over social networking sites.

In 2003, Gregg Easterbrook wrote *The Progress Paradox: How Life Gets Better While People Feel Worse*,[1] in which he explored the question of whether material prosperity contributed to a sense of individuals' well-being. One of the questions in the book was whether having more money and material objects resulted in people's happiness. Easterbrook found that having a sense of options may first contribute to someone's feeling of security, but once those new options were explored for their novelty, the person's happiness level returned to where it had been before he or she attained the new goods. The elusive nature of whether more technology actually contributes to a feeling of satisfaction has been difficult to measure, but one thing does seem certain: once we have technology, very few of us are willing to do without it. Despite the problems of using cell phones and the Internet—the annoyance of other peoples' calls, the risk of identity theft, and the continuous pressure to respond to instant messages 24/7—these technologies have already begun to contribute to long-term cultural changes that will inevitably continue to shape cultural values.

TECHNOLOGY, TIME, AND SPACE

As discussed, some technologies have a greater impact on issues of time and space than others. The analog clock imposed a way of thinking about time that was measured in units of sixty seconds, sixty minutes, and twenty-four hours as a means of measuring one day and night. When the electric light bulb was invented, illumination in the home and in public places changed the concept of day and night. Both the clock and electric light contributed to the growth of the industrial revolution that measured workers' time and productivity and changed the economic relationship between production and consumption of goods.

Electronic technologies such as the cell phone and the Internet do much the same thing. They change a person's sense of time, because they are available twenty-four hours a day, seven days a week. They give their users an illusion of control over their own activities, while reinforcing the idea that to be good cell phone or Internet users, we must respond quickly, or risk appearing disinterested in our work or in others.

The demand to always be "on"—whether online or on call—has introduced a level of technologically induced stress in our lives that has made many people feel compelled to respond quickly, even though they may respond incompletely or very briefly, using a shorthand style of communication. For many, responding, rather than communicating, has taken a toll on the quality of their interactions with others and on their sense of satisfaction about living or working in a social environment. No matter how often we use cell phones and the Internet, the basic need for human interaction is still a part of our culture, though many people seem to reject this need or divert it to the relationships they find in cyberspace.

The placeless nature of communicating on the Internet through cyberspace or by using cell phones that allow greater mobility and control over where someone uses them results in a disassociation from geographic place. The ability to use these technologies in nontraditional places, or to connect to others over spaces that can't even be comprehended because the sense of space is irrelevant, is a powerful influence over how people think of themselves in relationship to others. The feeling a person has, along with the illusion of control, can be both liberating for those who have any type of social anxiety or for those who live in conditions that don't support their needs for some types of interactions or communities, but at the same time, the instability of the relationships in cyberspace can be fleeting or transitory. Depending on the person's needs and desires, the fragmented, disassociated relationships may be somewhat fulfilling, or they may contribute to further alienation and loneliness.

The ability to deal with the characteristics of the technologies people use depends on how these people are socialized and what other technologies they use— including the types of technologies available to them and their comfort in learning to use them. When they feel that they have mastered a technology, they feel even greater control over their environments. These illusions of control contribute to the personal relationships that people begin to feel with their technologies, and lead to further reliance on them, despite any potential drawbacks, such as system failure or forgetting to charge batteries. While cell phones are, for the most part, thought about as highly personal technologies, using the Internet by cell phone or over laptop computers or PDAs changes an individual's relationship to traditional places that had already reflected a socially constructed set of appropriate behaviors.

BLURRING PUBLIC AND PRIVATE ACTIVITIES

The sense of mobility that small, portable devices give has now resulted in a period of time in which new behaviors are being tested and negotiated. When we use these technologies for personal reasons in public places, the contrast of what had been appropriate behavior in a personal place becomes a matter of public display. A spotlight is focused on entire social relationships and expectations for appropriate behavior.

At the same time, greater reliance on technologies that are consumed personally, rather than communally, becomes a challenge for institutions that had previously based their delivery models on serving the masses, rather than the individual members of a heterogeneous audience. Former media industries that have provided the "glue" that reflects and reinforces social culture have begun to explore delivering content to consumers to guarantee their dominance in a technologized world where potentially every user can become a content provider. Public activities, from making a phone call to shopping, have been reconstructed to target individual use rather than to serve a broader "public." Targeted advertising to individuals has reinforced the ideas that individuals matter more than social groups, and traditional social practices have attempted to find new ways of maintaining relationships and encouraging participation even though technologies make it easier for individuals to be disconnected from other people in real places in real time.

All of these changes are affecting generational cohorts differently, largely because habits play such an important role in helping people negotiate new technologies and practices. Peer groups are important social networks, and social learning over time conditions people to consider how willing they are to change traditional patterns of behavior. Lifestyles that change over a lifetime are important factors for how people maintain social relationships and how they manage the tasks that they must, to get through the day. New technologies have always favored the young, because they have not yet established a pattern of behavior that is so deeply entrenched that they don't have to "unlearn" behavioral patterns. For young users, mastery over new technologies is a matter of superiority over elders, and expertise is empowering. The characteristics of digital technologies accelerate traditional concepts of time; these technologies operate faster than the human mind, and they substitute information that is separated from its source for instant, fragmented, and incomplete data that meet the needs of a fast-paced culture for speed, rather than completeness or context. For all of these reasons, cell phones and the Internet remain powerful technologies to simultaneously give people an illusion of control over their lives and to make them feel that they are responding to a social imperative to use more technology in a more technologized world.

When comparing the use of cell phones and the Internet in the United States with the cultural changes that other countries are experiencing, the cultural change in the United States may appear to be happening at a snail's pace. Many other cultures are experiencing more dramatic changes than the United States, because wireless coverage can be more effective in small regions or small countries, and low-cost cell phones can revolutionize communication patterns in places that were not encumbered by established wired telephone infrastructures.

INTERNATIONAL COMPARISONS

The International Telecommunications Union (ITU) conducted a study in 1984 titled *The Missing Link*, in which it determined that at the time, there were approximately 600 million (wired) telephones in the world, but that two-thirds of the world's population had no access to a telephone at all.[2] While the growth of cell phones worldwide has not been steady or exponential, some regions have experienced very rapid diffusion of telephony in general and cell phones in particular, and in most cases, these countries are currently using 3G cell phones rather than the 2G phones that are most common in America. Access to the Internet is also changing throughout the world, largely because of the wireless systems that reduce the cost for expensive wired systems. In many regions the combination of cell phones, wireless communications, and links to Internet services has dramatically changed regional and national cultures.

In Japan, 3G phones enable full motion video, and commuters can watch entire films or television programs on their cell phones. In South Korea, where in the 1980s only one wired phone was in existence for every 600 people, 90 percent of the population now has wired phones, and three-quarters of them have 3G cell phones.[3]

In Saudi Arabia, where young males and females are kept apart, cell phones have allowed young people to have relationships with members of the opposite sex, date by phone, and even have phone sex, thus potentially changing gender relationships and religious law that is centuries old. Phones with camera features are illegal because they may be used to photograph women,[4] a violation of religious practice.

Cell phones have also been adapted in some parts of the world to reinforce cultural practices. In many Muslim countries, cell phone users have the option of using electronic reminders of when to pray and a directional service to orient them toward Mecca. In Taiwan, cell phones blessed at the Temple of Matsu are held in high regard.[5] Even some of the world's poorest people have embraced using cell phones for economic empowerment. The United Nations set a goal of having 50 percent of the poorest nations connected to a form of telephony by 2015, but already, 77 percent of the world's population lives within range of a wireless network, and people in many poorer countries have organized to share cell phones.[6]

A bevy of articles in recent issues of the *Economist* predict a great future for cell phones, opining that perhaps cell phones will be the engine of creating greater economic growth in the developing world: "When it comes to mobile phones, there is no need for intervention or funding from the UN: even the world's poorest people are already rushing to embrace mobile phones because their economic benefits are so apparent. Mobile phones do not rely on a permanent electricity supply and can be used by people who cannot read or write."[7]

In many third world nations that had no telephone service at all, cell phones have contributed to radically different communication practices. Many people in poor countries spend a larger proportion of their income on telecommunications than those in rich ones, because they realize what economic benefits can result from wireless communication forms. Farmers and fishermen can pool resources to use a cell phone to check official prices for their goods. In Bangladesh, the telephone ladies—those women who buy or rent a cell phone and charge others to make or receive calls—received attention when Muhammad Yunus won the 2006 Nobel Peace Prize for his system of offering "micro-loans" to poor people to empower them to engage in activities that could perhaps help lift them from poverty.

THE GLOBAL VILLAGE

The definition of a "global village" depends on the approach taken to describing what social arrangements constitute the conditions surrounding communication among individuals and groups of people. Samuel F. B. Morse, credited as the inventor of the telegraph, used the term when he envisioned a world with telegraph wires that would allow electronic communication over distances using his electronic "language" of dots and dashes called Morse code. Guglielmo Marconi, credited as the inventor of wireless radio, thought that wireless communication would allow everyone in the world to be a broadcaster as well as a receiver of radio signals. Marshall McLuhan, considered a prophet of the electronic age, thought more philosophically of how the combination of electronic media would link every region of the world through real-time satellite distribution of images and sounds that would return us to an electronically distributed form of oral communication. All of these visionaries used the term "global village" to describe their view of the world's future, with their own preferred technology as the hub around which all social life could thrive. Each of them had a good idea, but each was limited in the way he saw the world. What they did have in common, though, was the idea that each of their technologies could radically change time and space for their users. What they didn't realize was how their technologies would be developed and how they would ultimately radically redefine families, social groups, communities, religion, and every other social institution.

Morse, Marconi, and McLuhan, the alliterative trio of prognosticators who each thought they knew what the global village would be, were thinking technologically, if not socially. What seemed to be missing in each of their scenarios of the future was a sense of who could afford to use their chosen technologies, how expensive it would be to maintain an infrastructure of support, and finally, how their technologies would change over time. The new global village that is emerging uses technologies, but situates its similarities and its differences in the social realm.

In industrialized nations, most uses of cell phones and the Internet extend social networks and serve individuals rather than the masses. In third world nations, groups tend to work together with the cell phone or the Internet as a tool for empowerment. In the new global village, there is greater access to technology, even if it has to be shared or creatively distributed. What happens socially determines whether someone can have the opportunity to participate in village life, though much of that life is in cyberspace. The real future, then, of increasing reliance on cell phones and the Internet may well result in a global village that is not so much separated by social difference as it is united by the tools used for the members of the new global village.

Notes

Chapter 1

1. According to the FCC, as of November 2005, 92.9% of the homes in the United States had at least one traditional (not cell) telephone. U.S. Telecommunications: FCC Statistics, http://ustelecom.org/index.php?uh=home.news.telecom_stats, Sept. 22, 2006 (accessed October 28, 2006).

2. John Brooks chronicles the development of AT&T as an emerging giant in telephony and discusses the debates of radio inventors who experimented with wireless telephony in *Telephone: The First Hundred Years* (New York: Harper & Row, 1975), 140–142.

3. U.S. Telecommunications: FCC Statistics.

4. iMedia Connection, "Cell Phone Usage Continues to Rise," April 22, 2002, http://www.imediaconnection.com/global/5728.asp?ref+http://www.imediaconnection.com/7/5/2006 (accessed July 5, 2006).

5. National Public Radio, *Morning Edition*, December 11, 2006.

6. Andrew Kohut, "Truly a World Wide Web: Global Attitude Survey, 2005," *Pew Charitable Trusts*, February 21, 2005, http://www.pewtrusts.com/ideas/ideas_item.cfm?content_item_id=3257&content_type_id=7&issue_name=Society%20and%20the%20Internet&issue=10&page=7&name=Grantee%20Press%20 (accessed February 23, 2005).

7. Harris Interactive, "Almost Three-Quarters of all U.S. Adults—An Estimated 163 million—Go Online," *Harris Poll 40*, May 12, 2005, http://www.harrisinteractive.com/harris_poll/printerfriend/index.asp?PID=569 (accessed May 25, 2006).

8. Marshall McLuhan, *Understanding Media: The Extensions of Man* (New York: Signet, 1964).

9. Neil Postman, *Technopoly: The Surrender of Culture to Technology* (New York: Knopf, 1992).

10. The Luddites were a social movement in Great Britain during the nineteenth century. Possibly named for Ned Ludd, who destroyed machinery, the Luddites smashed machines because they feared the changes that would result in social life if the industrial revolution were allowed to spread. Today, a Luddite is someone who fears or distains technology.

11. Juliet B. Schor, *The Overworked American: The Unexpected Decline of Leisure* (New York: Basic Books, 1991), 1–2.

12. Lewis Mumford, *Technics and Human Development: The Myth of the Machine* (New York: Harcourt Brace Jovanovich, 1966).

13. Bernard Doray, *From Taylorism to Fordism: A Rational Madness*, trans. David Macey (London: Free Association Books, 1988).

14. Lance Strate, "Cybertime," in *Communication and Cyberspace: Social Interaction in an Electronic Environment*, ed. Lance Strate, Ron L. Jacobson, and Stephanie Gibson, 2nd ed. (Cresskill, NJ: Hampton Press, 2003), 364.

15. Edward T. Hall, *The Dance of Life: The Other Dimension of Time* (Garden City, NY: Anchor, 1984).

16. Jeremy Rifkin, *Time Wars: The Primary Conflict in Human History* (New York: Simon & Schuster, 1987), 19.

17. Ibid., 19

18. Joshua Meyerowitz, *No Sense of Place* (New York: Oxford University Press, 1985).

19. Ken Belson, "I Want to Be Alone. Please Call Me," *New York Times*, June 27, 2004, 14.

Chapter 2

1. Karen Riggs, *Granny @ Work* (New York: Routledge, 2004), 182–183. I'm indebted to Riggs for suggesting the generational framework that inspired my thoughts on audience identification and peer influence on using cell phones and the Internet. Since reading her work, I've seen the generations described in similar ways, though I don't know if she was the organizational genius behind the order. She does not address issues of the C generation in her work.

2. For a description of the research developed at the University of Chicago, see Robert E. L. Faris, *Chicago Sociology, 1920–1932* (Chicago: University of Chicago Press, 1970). The contributions of major researchers in the area can be found in "The Chicago School," in Everett M. Rogers' *A History of Communication Study* (New York: The Free Press, 1994), 137–202.

3. Carolyn Marvin, *When Old Technologies Were New* (New York: Oxford University Press, 1988), 5.

4. John Brooks, *Telephone: The First Hundred Years* (New York: Harper & Row, 1975), 40–43.

5. Erik Barnouw, *A Tower in Babel: A History of Broadcasting in the United States*, vol. 1, *1933* (New York: Oxford University Press, 1966), 210–211. Barnouw cites the 1927 patent of the dissector tube by Philo Farnsworth as important for the experimental nature of television broadcasting, and experiments in telecasting by Ernst F. W. Alexanderson, Edgar S. Love, and Vladimir Zworykin.

6. Claude S. Fischer, *America Calling: A Social History of the Telephone to 1940* (Berkeley: University of California Press, 1992).

7. As quoted by Fischer, 2.

8. H. M. Boettinger, *The Telephone Book* (Croton-on-Hudson, NY: Riverwood Press, 1977).

9. Linda Rosenkrantz, *Telegram!* (New York: Henry Holt & Co., 2003), 78, 120.

10. William H. Earle, "November 18, 1883: The Day Noon Showed Up on Time," *Smithsonian*, November 1983, 193–208.

11. Ithiel de Sola Poole, *Technologies of Freedom* (Cambridge, MA: Belknap Press, 1977).

12. Fischer, 66.

13. Marvin, 25.

14. Brooks, 8.

15. James Katz, *Connections* (New Brunswick, NJ: Transactions Publishers, 1999). See, in particular, 147–207.

16. For a complete analysis of the deregulation and divestiture, see Steve Coll, *The Deal of the Century: The Break-Up of AT&T* (New York: Athenaeum, 1986).

17. Paul Levinson, *Cellphone: The Story of the World's Most Mobile Medium and How It Has Transformed Everything* (New York: Palgrave Macmillan, 2004), 30.

18. Christos J. P. Moschovitis, Hilary Poole, Tami Schuyler, and Theresa M. Senft, *History of the Internet: A Chronology, 1843 to the Present* (Santa Barbara, CA: ABC-CLIO, Inc., 1999). This book provides a comprehensive examination of the people, innovations, and milestones in intellectual thought preceding the development of the Internet and includes an interesting cultural commentary on the contributions of these individuals. Grace Murray Hopper was a mathematician and officer in the U.S. Navy who programmed computers and who one day found a moth in one of the computer's electrical relays. She is responsible for coining the term "bug" in the system, though Moschovitis et al. attribute it to Thomas Edison (26–27). Licklider was a psychologist and computer scientist who had envisioned a system of time-sharing computers. He worked with ARPA scientists to connect individuals at different workstations to the mainframe computer (37). Cerf was a program manager at the Defense Advanced Research Projects Agency (DARPA) who contributed to standardization of network protocols (104), and Tim Berners-Lee, of CERN, developed the software for the

World Wide Web and hypertext transfer protocol (http) (162–164). See also James Gillies and Robert Cailliau, *How the Web Was Born* (Oxford: Oxford University Press, 2000).

19. Howard Reingold, *The Virtual Community: Homesteading on the Electronic Frontier* (New York: HarperPerennial, 1994), 66–67.

20. Sara Kiesler, "Preface" in *Culture of the Internet*, ed. Sara Kiesler (Mahwah, NJ: Lawrence Erlbaum, 1997), ix–x.

21. Sherry Turkle, "Hackers: Loving the Machine For Itself," in *The Second Self: Computers and the Human Spirit* (New York: Simon & Schuster, 1984), 196–238.

22. *PC Magazine*, 26 (1/2), November 7, 2006, cover.

23. While there are many histories of the radio industry, some examples of both innovation and social use can be found in Erik Barnouw's trilogy *A Tower in Babel: A History of Broadcasting in the United States to 1933* (New York: Oxford University Press, 1966), *The Golden Web: A History of Broadcasting in the United States, 1933–1953* (New York: Oxford University Press, 1968), and *The Image Empire: A History of Broadcasting in the United States from 1953* (New York: Oxford University Press, 1970).

24. Barnouw, *A Tower in Babel*, 144.

25. David Greenblatt, *The Call Heard Round the World* (New York: American Management Association, 2003), 66.

Chapter 3

1. *Time*, December 25, 2006, cover and 5.

2. Robert J. Samuelson, "A Cell Phone? Never for Me," MSNBC *Newsweek International*, August 23, 2005, http://www.msnbc.msn.com/id/5709348/site/newsweek (accessed September 12, 2005).

3. As quoted by Chris Anderson in "Welcome to the Broadband Home of the Future," *Wired*, 12 (11), November 2004, 11.

4. I'm indebted to Karen Riggs who set out the general generational descriptions for Matures, Boomers, and X and Y generations in *Granny @ Work* (New York: Routledge, 2004), 182–183.

5. Riggs, 183.

6. Titled Generation X from Douglas Coupland's *Generation X: Tales for an Accelerated Culture* (New York: St. Martin's Press, 1991).

7. "Generation C," Trendwatching, June 2004, http://www.trendwatching.com/trends/GENERATION_C.htm (accessed April 3, 2005).

8. Edward C. Baig, "Cell Phones Top Lists of What Gets Us Steamed," *USA Today*, August 3, 2006, http://www.usatoday.com/tech/news/2005-05-18-cell-phones-usat_x.htm (accessed August 5, 2006).

9. Rainie and Keeter, 11.

10. Carolyn Y. Johnson, "Do u txt ur kdz?" *Boston Sunday Globe*, December 17, 2006, A1, A20.

11. Yuki Noguchi and Kim Hart, "Teens Find a Ring Tone in a High-Pitched Repellent," *Washingtonpost.com*, June 14, 2006, DO1, http://www.washingtonpost.com/wp-dyn/content/article/2006/06/13/AR20061301557 (accessed June 14, 2006).

12. Harris Interactive: The Harris Poll 40 (May 12, 2005), http://www.harrisinteractive.com/harris_poll/printerfriend/index.asp?PID=569(accessed August 15, 2006).

13. DSL is the type of high-speed connection to the Internet that is furnished by the traditional telephone companies through telephone wires and cables. Broadband is a higher-capacity system that is offered by cable television companies. In 2005 the number of dial-up connections was approximately 34% in the United States, vs. 62% of a combination of broadband and DSL. Source: Pew Internet & American Life Project, http://www.pewinternet.org/trends/User_Demo_4.26.06.htm (accessed March 28, 2006).

14. Harris Interactive: The Harris Poll 40 May 12, 2005, http://www.harrisinteractive.com/harris_poll/printerfriend/index.asp?PID=569(accessed August 15, 2006).

15. As corroborated by Susannah Fox, "Digital Divisions," Pew Internet & American Life Project, October 5, 2005, 2, http://www.pewinternet.org/pdfs/PIP_Digital_Divisions_Oct_5_2005.pdf (accessed October 6, 2005).

16. Ibid., 2.

17. Ibid., 3.

18. Ibid., 3–4

Chapter 4

1. While Marshall McLuhan's ideas about "sense ratios" can be found in much of his work, a good description of McLuhan's work on embodiment can be found in Raymond Gozzi, Jr., "Why Print Is 'Cool' and Orality Is Body Temperature," in *The Legacy of McLuhan,* ed. Lance Strate and Edward Wachtel (Cresskill, NJ: Hampton Press, 2005), 219–225.

2. Many contemporary laptop manufacturers use the thumb scan as a security device for users; the person's thumb is used as an identifier of the person attempting to open a programs.

3. Jeffrey Selingo, "Hey Kid, Your Backpack Is Ringing," *New York Times*, March 18, 2004, E1, E6.

4. Carl Sagan, *Dragons of Eden: Speculations on the Evolution of Human Intelligence* (New York: Random House, 1977), 8.

5. "The State of the News Media 2004," *The Project for Excellence in Journalism* Journalism.org, May 2004, http://www.stateofthenewsmedia.org (accessed March 28, 2004).

6. Hassan Fattah, "America Untethered," *American Demographics*, March 2003, 35–39.

7. Jason Fry, "When Talk Isn't Cheap: Is Emailing Colleagues Who Sit Feet Away a Sign of Office Dysfunction, or a Wise Move?" *Wall Street Journal*, November 28, 2005, 1.

8. James Beniger, "Who Shall Control Cyberspace," in *Communication and Cyberspace*, 2nd ed., ed. Lance Strate, Ron L. Jacobson, and Stephanie Gibson (Cresskill, NJ: Hampton Press, 2003), 61.

9. American Psychological Association, "Internet Addiction Gains Attention as It Intersects with Other Problems," *Alcoholism & Drug Abuse Weekly* 18, no. 33 (2006): 1–7.

10. Joel Conarroe, "Addicted to Talking," *New York Times*, August 5, 2000, A15.

11. Lee Rainie and Scott Keeter, "Pew Internet Project Data Memo: Cell Phone Use," Pew Internet & American Life Project, April 2006, 1, http://www.pewinternet. org/pdfs/PIP_Cell_phone_study.pdf (accessed May 11, 2006).

12. See, for example, Gert-Jan Meerk, Regina J. J. M. van den Eijnden, and Henk F. L. Garretse, "Predicting Compulsive Internet Use: It's All about Sex!" *CyberPsychology & Behavior* 9, no. 2 (February 2006): 95–103. The researchers conducted an online questionnaire with Internet users. They found that gaming and erotica were the most important applications of the Internet for compulsive Internet users.

13. L. S. Whang, S. Lee, and G. Chang, "Internet Over-Users' Psychological Profiles: A Behavior Sampling Analysis on Internet Addiction," *CyberPsychology & Behavior* 6, no. 2 (2003): 143–150.

14. Kimberly S. Young, *Caught in the Net: How to Recognize the Signs of Internet Addiction—And a Winning Strategy for Recovery* (New York: John Wiley & Sons, 1998), 20–21; other researchers who have written about the psychological profiles of Internet overusers, or addicts, are A. J. Campbell, S. R. Cummings, S. R. Hughes, "Internet Use of the Socially Fearful: Addiction or Therapy?" *CyberPsychology & Behavior* 9, no. 2 (February 2006): 69–81, and C. Chou, L. Dondron, and J. Belland, "A Review of the Research on Internet Addiction," *Educational Psychology Review* 17, no. 6 (December 2005): 363–388.

15. Young, 179.

16. Ibid., 174. The impact of additive behaviors in schools has also been confirmed by B. D. Ng and P. Wiemer-Hastings in "Addiction to the Internet and Online Gaming," *CyberPscyhology & Behavior* 8, no. 2, 2005, 110–113.

17. Elizabeth Millard, "The Future of Online Gambling," *E-Commerce Times*, October 23, 2003, http://www.ecommercetimes.com/story/31962.html (accessed October 29, 2006), and Kate Norton and Mark Scott, "Online Gambling Hedges Its U.S. Bets,"

Business Week Online, August 22, 2006, 1, http://businessweekonline/Onlingambling/26.08.22.06 (accessed September 28, 2006).

18. Millard, citing Forrester analyst Chris Charron.

19. Matt Richtel, "Wall St. Bets on Gambling on the Web," *New York Times*, December 25, 2005, B25. According to Richtel, some of America's top investment firms, such as Fidelity, Morgan Stanley, Merrill Lynch, and Goldman Sachs hold shares in mutual funds that reflect gambling operations offshore. When asked about the legality of these investments, a spokesperson for one house said, "Our analysis shows the gain from these stocks outweighs the very small risk."

20. "Internet Gambling May Indicate More Serious Problem," *Alcoholism & Drug Abuse Weekly*, March 25, 2002, 6.

21. Will Wright, "Dream Machines," *Wired*, April 2006, 111–112, from a special section on gaming, 108–149.

22. Ibid., 108.

23. Examples of pro-social games include things like *Nintendogs*, which allows children to care for virtual puppies, and 3-D games, like *Second Life*.

24. Wright, 112.

25. John C. Beck and Mitchell Wade, *Got Game: How the Gamer Generation Is Reshaping Business Forever* (Boston, MA: Harvard Business School Press, 2004), 3.

26. Gloria Goodale, "Video-Game Industry Mulls over the Future beyond Shoot-'em-ups," *Christian Science Monitor*, June 3, 2005, 11.

27. Beck and Wade, 19.

Chapter 5

1. The images of the UCLA student and the Abu Ghraib prisoner pictures were both taken with digital cameras and uploaded on the Internet. The pictures of Saddam Hussein's execution and the London bombing were taken by people with cell phones and uploaded on the Internet.

2. Robert W. McChesney, *Corporate Media and the Threat to Democracy* (New York: Seven Stories Press, 1997), 5.

3. Mark S. Fowler and Daniel L Brenner, "A Marketplace Approach to Broadcast Regulation," *Texas Law Review* 60, no. 2 (February 1988): 209–257.

4. The figure of 39% was the result of a compromise during the 2004 controversy in which the then chief commissioner Michael Powell hoped to allow each media owner to control up to 45% of the media within a market.

5. In a personal conversation with Mark Fowler in 2001, Mr. Fowler admitted that he still believed in the theory behind marketplace rules, but that the problem was the number of lobbyists in Washington, DC, who had diverted the mission from opening the field to competition to favoring the powerful media organizations.

6. Bill Moyers, "Media and Democracy," *Nation*, December 1, 2003, http://www.thenation.com/mhtml?=20031215&s=moyers (accessed February 4, 2005).

7. Al Gore reportedly coined the term the "information superhighway" in 1994 while describing the Clinton/Gore agenda to update communication networks throughout the nation.

8. Al Gore, "Al Gore's Code Red," *AlterNet*, October 6, 2005, http://www.alternet.org/story/26494 (accessed October 7, 2005).

9. Matt Drudge, *Drudge Report,* January 14, 1998, http://www.drudgereport.com/ml.htm (accessed December 2, 2006).

10. Corey Pein, "Blog-gate," *Columbia Journalism Review* 44 no. 2 (March 2005): 22–28.

11. Andrew Sullivan, "The Blogging Revolution: Weblogs Are to Words What Napster Was to Music," *Wired*, May 2002, 12–14, http://wired.com/wired/archive/10.05/mustread.html? (accessed November 19, 2006).

12. Graph citing Technorati statistics in Andrew P. Madden, "The Business of Blogging," *Technology Review* 108, no. 8 (August 2005): 37.

13. Literature on information overload and using media to confirm one's own thoughts is extensive; see, for example, Jarice Hanson, *Connections: Technologies of Communication* (New York: HarperCollins, 1994), 46.

14. Cass Sunstein, "Is the Internet Really a Blessing for Democracy? *Boston Review: The Daily We*, http://bostonreview.mit.edu/BR26.3/sunstein.html (accessed August 15, 2002).

15. Amanda Lenhart and Susannah Fox, "Bloggers: A Portrait of the Internet's New Storytellers," Pew Internet & American Life Project, July 19, 2006, iv, 1, http://www.pewinternet.org/ (accessed July 20, 2006).

16. Madden, 37.

17. Adam Curry, "Cool to Hear My Own Audio-Blog," October 21, 2002, http://radio.weblogs.com/0001014/200310/12.html#a4604 (accessed March 23, 2006).

18. Andrew P. Madden, "Is There a Business in Blogging?" *Technology Review* 108, no. 8 (August 2005): 36–38.

19. Barb Palser, "Hype or the Real Deal?" *American Journalism Review* (February/March 2006): 65.

20. Robert MacMillan, "The Paradox of Podcasting," August 11, 2005, http://www.washingtonpost.com/wp-dyn/content/article/2005/08/11/AR2005081100695. p. 2. (accessed August 11, 2005).

21. Palser, 65.

22. Kevin Bullis, "Podcasting Takes Off," *Technology Review* 108, no. 5 (October 2005): 30.

23. Chris Gaither, "Chat from the War Zone," *New York Times*, September 12, 2005, A1.

24. John Hockenberry, "The Blogs of War," *Wired*, August 2005, 118–123, 134–136.

25. Deborah Potter, "iPod, You Pod, We All Pod," *American Journalism Review* 28 no. 1 (February/March 2006): 64.

26. Charles C. Mann, "Spam + Blogs = Trouble," *Wired*, September 2006, 104–115. See 106.

27. Electronic Freedom Forum, "EFF: Fighting for Bloggers' Rights," http://www.eff.org/bloggers/ (accessed October 10, 2005). See the EFF Web site for more projects undertaken by the organization for a variety of purposes, including copyright, anonymity, censorship, and digital rights management, to name a few: www.eff.org.

28. Thomas B. Edsall, "FEC Rules Exempt Blogs From Internet Political Limits," Washingtonpost.com, March 28, 2006, A03, http://www.washingtonpost.com/wp-dyn/content/article/2006/03/27/AR2006032701474.html (accessed March 28, 2006).

29. Will Lester, "Cell-Phone-Only Crowd May Alter Polling," *Yahoo News*, May 15, 2006, http://news.yahoo.com/s/ap/20060515/ap_on_re_us/polling_predicament (accessed May 16, 2006).

Chapter 6

1. Lori Gottlieb, "How Do I Love Thee?" *Atlantic Monthly*, March 2006, 58–59.

2. Ibid., 63.

3. Mary Madden and Amanda Lenhart, "Online Dating," *Pew American Life and Society*, March 5, 2006, 2, http://wwwpewinternet.org/pdfs/PIP_Online_Dating.pdf (accessed April 12, 2006).

4. Dore Hollander, "Among Young Adults, Use of the Internet to Find Sexual Partners Is Rising," *Perspectives on Sexual and Reproductive Health* 34, no. 6 (November/December 2002), 318–319.

5. Beatriz Lia and Avila Mileham, "Online Infidelity in Internet Chat Rooms: An Ethnographic Exploration," *Computers in Human Behavior* 23, no. 1 (January 2007): 11–31.

6. Michael W. Ross, "Typing, Doing, and Being: Sexuality and the Internet," *Journal of Sex Research* 42, no. 4 (November 2005): 342–352.

7. Andrea M. Bergstrom, "New Approaches to Dating and Relationships in the Information Society" (unpublished manuscript), December 3, 2005, 10.

8. Ibid., 14.

9. David Knox, Lakisha Sturdivant, and Marty E. Zusman, "College Student Use of the Internet for Mate Selection," *College Student Journal* 35, no. 1 (June 2001): 158–159.

10. John Cassidy, "Me Media," *New Yorker*, May 15, 2006, 50–60.

11. Ibid., 52.

12. See, for example, "How to Catch a Humbert," *New Statesman*, July 31, 2006, 48–49, and Jia Lynn Yang, "Can This Man Make MySpace Safe for Kids?" *Fortune*, July 20, 2006, 32.

13. Diana G. Oblinger and Brian Hawkins, "The Myth about Putting Information Online," *Educause Review*, 41, no. 5 (September/October): 2006, 14–15.

14. Michael R. Fancher, "Social-Networking Sites Pose Ethical Concerns," *Seattle Times*, August 20, 2006, A21.

15. Simson Garfinkle, *Database Nation: The Death of Privacy in the 21st Century* (New York: O'Reilly, 2000).

16. Adam Penenberg, "Is Google Evil?" *Valley Advocate*, January 4–10, 2006, 15.

17. "Will a Hacker Crash Your Cell Phone?" *WinXPnews*, E-Zine, 4, no. 48, December 7, 2004, http://www winxpnews.com/?id+154 (accessed December 7, 2004).

18. Brian Krebs, "Alarming Phishing Trends," *WashingtonPost.com*, February 22, 2006, http://blog. Washingtonpost.com/securityfix/2006 02/alarming-phishing-trends.html (accessed February 23, 2006).

19. Toby Lester, "The Reinvention of Privacy," *Atlantic Monthly*, March 2001, 27–39.

20. Laura M. Holson, "Disney Phone Service Has Parents in Mind, *New York Times*, April 5, 2007, A1.

21. John Powers, "Can We Talk?" *Boston Globe Magazine*, February 8, 2004, l, 16, 24–26, 31–32.

Chapter 7

1. For more about agenda setting and how media set agendas, see Joseph Turow, *Media Today: An Introduction to Mass Communication* (Boston, MA: Houghton Mifflin, 2003), 138–139.

2. Marshall Poe, "The Hive," *Atlantic Monthly*, September, 2006, 86–94; see 86.

3. Ibid., 88–89.

4. Stacy Schiff, "Know It All," *New Yorker*, July 31, 2006, 36, 38–43; see 38.

5. Shawn Fanning created the original Napster program to allow peer-to-peer sharing of files, and MP3 programs were accessible free, over the Internet. After a protracted legal dispute, Fanning gave up Napster and repositioned his music sharing system to a legal, pay-per-service model, which was eventually bought by one of the major music distribution companies.

6. James Fallows, "File Not Found," *Atlantic Monthly*, September 2006, 142, 144145.

7. Ibid., 142.

8. Simson Garfinkle, "Confessions of a Scan Artist," *Technology Review* 109, no. 2 (March/April 2006): 78–79.

9. Robert MacMillan, "Cell Phone Camera Fazes Flasher," Washingtonpost.com, August 30, 2005, http://www.washingtonpost.com/wp-dyn/content/article/2005/08/30/AR2005083000574.html (accessed August 30, 2005).

10. "Thanks to Cellphones, TV Screens Get Smaller," *Wilmington Star*, (Wilmington, DE), *Starnewsonline.com*, February 15, 2005, http://www.wilmingtonstar.com/apps/pbcs.dll/article?AID=/20050215/ZNYT05/50215038 (accessed February 16, 2005).

11. "Thanks to Cellphones," 2.

12. Zizi Papacharissi and Jan Fernback, "Online Privacy and Consumer Protection: An Analysis of Portal Privacy Statements," *Journal of Broadcasting & Electronic Media* 49, no. 3 (September 2005): 259–281.

13. Barb Palser, "Artful Disguises," *American Journalism Review* 28, no. 5, (October/November 2006): 90.

14. N. Abramovitz and Guilio A. De Leo, "PARTY ON, DUDES! Ignorance Is the Curse of the Information Age," *American Spectator* 35, no. 5 (March/April 2002): 68–71.

15. David Talbot, "The Internet Is Broken," *Technology Review* 108, no. 11 (December 2005/January 2006): 63–69.

16. Ibid., 63.

Chapter 8

1. Ashley Simonsen, "Death of the Payphone?" *Regional Review* 13, no. 3 2003: 2–3.

2. Jennifer Pendleton, "Thirty and Counting," *Emmy*, February 2006, 192.

3. Greg Hernandez, "The 'Anytime, Anywhere' Online TV Trend," *E-Commerce News*, October 28, 2006, http://www.ecommercetimes.com/story/53951.html (accessed October 29, 2006).

4. "To Infinity and Beyond," *Economist: A Survey of Television*, April 13, 2002, 8.

5. Eric Taub, "Cell Theory," *Emmy*, February 2006, 54.

6. Jane Black, "A Bad, Sad Hollywood Ending?" *BusinessWeekOnline*, May 16, 2002, http://www.Businessweek.com/technology/content/may2002/tc20020515_8741.htm (accessed April 4, 2006).

7. Ibid., 2.

8. Matt Brady, "How Digital Animation Conquered Hollywood," *Wired*, March 2006, 119.

9. "Report: Online Newspaper Readership Up 11% in October," *Editor & Publisher Online*, November 15, 2005, http://wwweditorandpublisher.com/eandp/news/article_display.jsp?vnu_content_id=1001480273 (accessed November 16, 2005).

10. Carl Session Stepp, "Why Do People Read Newspapers?" *American Journalism Review* 26 no. 1, December/January (2004): 34–39.

11. As quoted by Betsey Streisand and Richard J. Newman, "The New Media Elites," *U.S. News & World Report* (November 14, 2005): 54–62.

12. Alison Lobron, "Wi-Fi Wars: On One Side: Laptop Users, On the Other Side: Café Owners," *Boston Sunday Globe*, July 9, 2006, B1, B3.

13. See, for example, Gary Gumpert, *Talking Tombstones, and Other Tales of the Media Age* (New York: Oxford University Press, 1987), and Susan J. Drucker and Gary Gumpert, (eds., *Voices in the Street: Explorations in Gender, Media, and Public Space* (Cresskill, NJ: Hampton Press, 1997).

14. Pui-Wing Tam and Mylene Mangalindan, "Cyber Monday' Sales Strong, Web Sites Say," *Wall Street Journal*, Eastern Edition, November 29, 2005, B1, B-9.

15. John C. Beck and Mitchell Wade, *Got Game: How the Gamer Generation Is Reshaping Business Forever* (Boston, MA: Harvard Business School Press, 2004), 9.

16. Ibid., 11–22.

Chapter 9

1. Gregg Easterbrook, *The Progress Paradox: How Life Gets Better While People Feel Worse* (New York: Random House, 2003).

2. "The Device That Ate Everything," *Economist*, March 12–18, 2005, 22.

3. "Behind the Digital Divide," *Economist*, March 12–18, 2005, 25.

4. "Islamic Dilemma," *National Geographic*, April 2005, 13.

5. "Technology Quarterly," *Economist*, March 12–18, 2005, 12–15.

6. "Calling Across the Divide," *Economist*, March 12–18, 2005, 74.

7. "Technology Quarterly," 15.

Selected Bibliography

Anderson, Chris. *The Long Tail: Why the Future of Business Is Selling Less of More*. New York: Hyperion, 2006.

Barnouw, Erik. *A Tower in Babel: A History of Broadcasting in the United States*. Volume 1: *1933*. New York: Oxford University Press, 1966.

Beck, John C., and Mitchell Wade. *Got Game: How the Gamer Generation Is Reshaping Business Forever*. Boston, MA: Harvard Business School Press, 2004.

Boettinger, H. M. *The Telephone Book*. Croton-on-Hudson, New York: Riverwood Press, 1977.

Brooks, John. *Telephone: The First Hundred Years*. New York: Harper & Row, 1975.

Coll, Steve. *The Deal of the Century: The Break-Up of AT&T*. New York: Athenaeum, 1986.

Doray, Bernard (David Macey, trans.). *From Taylorism to Fordism: A Rational Madness*. London: Free Association Books, 1988.

Easterbrook, Gregg. *The Progress Paradox: How Life Gets Better While People Feel Worse*. New York: Random House, 2003.

Faris, Robert E. L. *Chicago Sociology 1920–1932*. Chicago: University of Chicago Press, 1970.

Fischer, Claude S. *America Calling: A Social History of the Telephone to 1940*. Berkeley: University of California Press, 1992.

Fowler, Mark S., and Daniel L Brenner. "A Marketplace Approach to Broadcast Regulation." *Texas Law Review* 60(2), February 1988: 209–257.

Fox, Susannah. "Digital Divisions." *Pew Internet & American Life Project*. October 5, 2005, http://www.pewinternet.org/pdfs/PIP_Digital_Divisions_Oct_5_2005.pdf (accessed October 6, 2005).

Garfinkle, Simson. *Database Nation: The Death of Privacy in the 21st Century*. New York: O'Reilly, 2000.

Hall, Edward T. *The Dance of Life: The Other Dimension of Time*. Garden City, NY: Anchor, 1984.

James Katz. *Connections: Social and Cultural Studies of the Telephone in American Life*. New Brunswick, NJ: Transaction Press, 1999.

Kiesler, Sara (ed.). *Culture of the Internet*. Mahwah, NJ: Lawrence Erlbaum Associates, 1997.

Kohut, Andrew. "Truly a World Wide Web: Global Attitude Survey, 2005." *Pew Charitable Trusts*. February 21, 2005, http://www.pewtrusts.com/ideas/ ideas_item.cfm?content_item_id=3257&content_type_id=7&issue_name= Society%20and%20the%20Internet&issue=10&page=7&name=Grantee %20Press%20(accessed February 23, 2005).

Lenhart, Amanda, and Susannah Fox. "Bloggers: A Portrait of the Internet's New Storytellers." *Pew Internet & American Life Project*, July 19, 2006, http://www. pewinternet.org/ (accessed July 20, 2006).

Levinson, Paul. *Cellphone: The Story of the World's Most Mobile Medium and How It Has Transformed Everything*. New York: Palgrave Macmillan, 2004.

Madden, Mary, and Amanda Lenhart. "Online Dating." *Pew American Life and Society*. March 5, 2006, http://wwwpewinternet.org/pdfs/PIP_Online_Dating.pdf (accessed April 12, 2006).

Marvin, Carolyn. *When Old Technologies Were New*. New York: Oxford University Press, 1988.

McChesney, Robert W. *Corporate Media and the Threat to Democracy*. New York: Seven Stories Press, 1997.

McLuhan, Marshall. *Understanding Media: The Extensions of Man*. New York: Signet, 1964.

Meerk, Gert-Jan, Regina J. J. M. van den Eijnden, and Henk F. L. Garretse. "Predicting Compulsive Internet Use: It's All about Sex!" *CyberPsychology & Behavior*, 9(1), February 2006: 95–103.

Meyerowitz, Joshua. *No Sense of Place*. New York: Oxford University Press, 1985.

Moschovitis, Christos J. P., Hilary Poole, Tami Schuyler, and Theresa M. Senft. *History of the Internet: A Chronology, 1843 to the Present*. Santa Barbara, CA: ABC-CLIO, Inc., 1999.

Mumford, Lewis. *Technics and Civilization*. New York: Harcourt, Brace & World, Inc., 1934.

———. *Technics and Human Development: The Myth of the Machine*. New York: Harcourt Brace Jovanovich, 1966.

Postman, Neil. *Technopoly: The Surrender of Culture to Technology*. New York: Alfred A. Knopf, 1992.

Rainie, Lee, and Scott Keeter. "Cell Phone Use." *Pew Internet & American Life Project*. April 3, 2006, www.pewinternet.org/pdf/PIP_Internet_Impact.pdf (accessed April 26, 2006).

Rifkin, Jeremy. *Time Wars: The Primary Conflict in Human History*. New York: Simon & Schuster, 1987.

Riggs, Karen. *Granny @ Work: Aging and New Technology on the Job in America*. New York: Routledge, 2004.

Rogers, Everett M. *A History of Communication Study*. New York: Free Press, 1994.

Rosenkrantz, Linda. *Telegram!* New York: Henry Holt & Co., 2003.

Ross, Michael W. "Typing, Doing, and Being: Sexuality and the Internet." *Journal of Sex Research* 42(4), November 2005: 342–352.

Schor, Juliet B. *The Overworked American: The Unexpected Decline of Leisure*. New York: Basic Books, 1991.

The State of the News Media 2004. *The Project for Excellence in Journalism*. Journalism.org, May 2004, http://www.stateofthenewsmedia.org (accessed March 28, 2004).

Strate, Lance. "Cybertime." In Lance Strate, Ron L. Jacobson, and Stephanie Gibson, (eds.), *Communication and Cyberspace: Social Interaction in an Electronic Environment*. 2nd ed. Cresskill, NJ: Hampton Press, 2003.

Turkle, Sherry. *The Second Self: Computers and the Human Spirit*. New York: Simon & Schuster, 1984.

U.S. Telecommunications: *FCC Statistics*, September 22, 2006, http://ustelecom.org/index.php?uh=home.news.telecom_stats (accessed October 28, 2006).

Whang, Leo Sang-Min, Sujuin Lee, and Geunyoung Chang. "Internet Over-Users' Psychological Profiles: A Behavior Sampling Analysis on Internet Addiction." *CyberPsychology & Behavior*, 6(2), 2003:143–150.

Young, Kimberly S. *Caught in the Net: How to Recognize the Signs of Internet Addiction— And a Winning Strategy for Recovery*. New York: John Wiley & Sons, 1998.

Index

CERN (European Organization for Nuclear Research) (trans.), 26, 135–36 n.18

Chat rooms: personals, 83; sex chat rooms, 59

Chemistry.com. *See* Social networking

Chicago School of Sociology, 18

Clock time, 9, 49–51, 126

Computers, 3; computer dating services, 81–88

Connaroe, Joel, 57–58

Control, illusions of control, 49

Conversation, changes in, 91–93, 123–24

Copyright, 37, 102; copyright laws, 102–4. *See also* DRM

Cultural history, components of, 17–20

Cyberspace: as a concept, 11; cyber communities, 114, 120–22; cybersexuality, 84; and place, 56; space-shifting, 56–57. *See also* Placelessness

Daily Show with Jon Stewart, 109

DeLeo, Guilio A., 112

Deregulation: of AT&T, 19, 24; of media industries, 67–69

De Sola Poole, Ithiel, 22

Digital divide, definition, 33–34

Digital logic, 47

Digital Millennium Copyright Act, 103–5, 109

Digital time, 44, 53

Disney: animation, 117; cell phones for children, 90–91

Do not call registry, 24

Doray, Bernard, 9

DRM (Digital rights management), 104–7; inducement, 105

DSL (Digital subscriber line): in homes, 3–4; percentage in homes, 137 n.13; speed of access, 44

Easterbrook, Gregg, 126

EEF (Electronic Freedom Forum), 76

E-Harmony, 82–83. *See also* Social networking

E-mail: habits, 3; behaviors, 54–55

Etiquette: cell phone, 13–14; social networking, 87–88

Exsosomatic information processing, 53

Facebook, 45, 86–87; thefacebook.com, 86

Fallows, James, 106

Fantasy life: in gaming, 62; and intimacy, 84; in sex chat rooms, 59

FCC (Federal Communications Commission), 29, 66–67

Film industry and change, 117

First Amendment, 66, 76

Fischer, Claude S., 22

Fowler, Mark, and deregulation, 68, 139 n.3

Fox, Susannah, 43, 46

Fragmented thinking, 95, 97–98; and self-expression, 123–24

FRC (Federal Radio Commission), 29

Friendster, 45, 86–87

Gambling, 59–61; worldwide, 60

Gaming, 59–63. *See also* Video gaming

Garfinkle, Simson, 88, 106

Gates, Bill, 26

Generation C: blogging, 71; characteristics of, 36–37; communication protocols, 45; digital thinking, 47; gaming, 62; instant messaging, 45; manipulating content, 110; marketing to, 51; personalization of cell phones, 37–38, 42; reliance on Internet for news, 97; time and space, 63

Generation X, 18; blogging, 71; characteristics of, 36; digital thinking,

Third-generation cell phones, 25, 129
Time magazine, 33
Timeshifting, 116
TiVo, 116
Treo, 1, 29
Turkle, Sherry, 27. *See also* Hackers

Valenti, Jack, 117
Video gaming, 59–63
Virtual communities. *See* Cyberspace
VoIP (Voice over Internet Protocol), 29–31, 114–15. *See also* IP telephony

Wade, Mitchell, 62–63, 122–23
Wales, Jimmy, 99
Web 2.0, 27, 76

Wikipedia, 98–100; WikiGnomes, 99; WikiTrolls, 99–100. *See also* Open source movement
Winklevoss, Cameron, 86
Winklevoss, Tyler, 86
Wireless telephone, 2
Women in the workforce, 23
Wright, Will, 61
WWW (World Wide Web), 26

Yahoo!, 83
Yanowitch, Richard, 119
Young, Kimberly S., 58–59. *See also* Addiction
YouTube, acquisition by Google, 3

Zuckerberg, Mark, 86–87
Zusman, Marty E., 86

About the Author

JARICE HANSON is Professor of Communication at the University of Massachusetts, Amherst, and Verizon Chair in Telecommunications at the School of Communications and Theater at Temple University in Philadelphia. She is the author/editor of seventeen books.